Clairvoyance

Easy Techniques to Enhance Your
Psychic Visions

*(The Ultimate Guide to Aura Reading and Other
Psychic Abilities)*

Kathy Massie

Published By **Andrew Zen**

Kathy Massie

All Rights Reserved

Clairvoyance: Easy Techniques to Enhance Your Psychic Visions (The Ultimate Guide to Aura Reading and Other Psychic Abilities)

ISBN 978-1-77485-631-4

No part of this guidebook shall be reproduced in any form without permission in writing from the publisher except in the case of brief quotations embodied in critical articles or reviews.

Legal & Disclaimer

The information contained in this ebook is not designed to replace or take the place of any form of medicine or professional medical advice. The information in this ebook has been provided for educational & entertainment purposes only.

The information contained in this book has been compiled from sources deemed reliable, and it is accurate to the best of the Author's knowledge; however, the Author cannot guarantee its accuracy and validity and cannot be held liable for any errors or omissions. Changes are periodically made to this book. You must consult your doctor or get professional medical advice before using any of the suggested remedies, techniques, or information in this book.

Upon using the information contained in this book, you agree to hold harmless the Author from and against any damages, costs, and expenses, including any legal fees potentially resulting from the application of any of the information provided by this guide. This disclaimer applies to any damages or injury caused by the use and application, whether directly or indirectly, of any advice or information presented, whether for breach of contract, tort, negligence, personal injury, criminal intent, or under any other cause of action.

You agree to accept all risks of using the information presented inside this book. You need to consult a professional medical practitioner in order to ensure you are both able and healthy enough to participate in this program.

TABLE OF CONTENTS

Introduction 1

Chapter 1: The Psychic 3

Chapter 2: Scientists Are Saying About Mind Reading 10

Chapter 3: Empathy And The Way It Works In Mind Reading 17

Chapter 4: People Who Naturally Read Minds 24

Chapter 5: Tips From Professional Mind Readers 28

Chapter 6: Activities To Enhance Your Mind-Reading Skills 36

Chapter 7: Preparing To Give Readings .. 41

Chapter 8: Readings 49

Chapter 9: Responsibilities That Are Part Of Being A Psychic 56

Chapter 10: Learning Your Psychic Powers 61

Chapter 11: Using Suggestion 68

Chapter 12: Communicating With The Dead 73

Chapter 13: Support For Mind Readers.. 79

Chapter 14: Developing Clairvoyance Exercises 86

Chapter 15: Guerilla Meditation 126

Chapter 16: Understanding Psychic Empaths................ 171

Conclusion 181

Introduction

If you are a fan of TV shows where a mind reader utilized to determine certain facts it is hard to believe that this really is feasible. It might surprise you to discover that the science is proving in support of every human being being capable to read minds. The majority of people aren't proficient at this skill however, it doesn't mean that it's not present. It's a skill that needs to be refined. This book is a guide to that part of thought and helps you understand someone else's mind, and teaches you how.

The problem that people have when trying to read minds is because they've not yet learned and perfected the abilities required. Once these skills are established as ones that are tapped any person's minds of those in their surroundings. In the television series "The Mentalist" viewers watched Patrick Jane helping police to find the root of criminals. He was previously engaged in psychic work that abused individuals, but was able to develop the capability to see minds which proved to be an extremely valuable one. We all have this ability but until you know how to utilize it, it's not useful to you.

Imagine being able and able to please others around you by anticipating their requirements. Imagine breaking the male-female divide and being capable of understanding the other gender. It's possible, however you have to invest some time in it since this isn't a ability that can be developed over night. Some claim that it can be learned in just a few minutes, but that's not likely. It takes time to master the skills. If you would like to utilize your psychic powers, you must be patient to learn.

But, your actions all through your life could hinder your capability. In the crowded world which we live, many have lost the ability to utilize the instincts of their bodies and get those instincts to pay off in the sense they are correct. It can take a while to build this confidence however, once you do get it, you'll have the ability to understand minds of people and create an enlightened lifestyle.

It's worth a try?

Chapter 1: The Psychic

What psychics can do that you may not be able to is detect emotions which is a useful instrument. They can discern from watching someone's attitude is and it's an excellent indicator of the characteristics listed above along with many other.

Fear

Dread

Empathy

Impatience

These are all crucial aspects when it comes to reading a person's mind. A psychic understands the importance of cleaning the mind of any clutter. If your brain is filled with thoughts of its own what is the chance that it ever going to take in thoughts of other people? It's a fact that those who don't believe that they are able to discern thoughts will probably never be able to because their belief has become so strong, their mental processes simply dismiss it as an unlikely possibility and then be in a state of denial that it's never happening.

What psychics say is to let your mind go. The method used to achieve this may differ. You might find that relaxation sessions are beneficial, where you take your thoughts off and focus on a particular area, or close your eyes and focus on breathing.

What is the reason you require an empty mind to go about mind reading?

It will make you more open to those around you and , consequently, more adept at recognizing their thoughts patterns. You might have observed the fact that Patrick Jane had a tendency to in the show, to lay on the couch and not do anything, with his eyes shut. This was due to a legitimate reason. If your mind is constantly bombarded by visual stimuli and mental thoughts all constantly, you'll be not as responsive. There's a limit to what you can think about in your brain, and if you're overflowing with stimuli you're not likely to to hear thoughts of others.

It is said blind people have a better understanding of what's happening around them than people who are sighted. There's a good reason behind this. They must develop their other senses to make up for the loss of sight. The senses you may not have experienced are the ones that you must focus on. Be aware of all things. Your feelings should be able to discern from other people the way they feel and express their anger, emotions, their happiness and so you can get an idea of who they are. This isn't an artifact. It's a highly empathetic feeling that you don't have yet developed, but must develop be able to develop if you wish to be able to read minds. You should be able to smell the scents around you as well as the auras of the people you interact with and the atmosphere at a home, and the atmosphere of the place you're put in. The development of your senses is vital to success in the field of thinking in a way that is readable.

Beyond what you can physically perceive

If you are looking at another person, truly look them up. Pay attention enough to tell you who the person is. There are clues to be found throughout the day. The ability to observe is essential to keep your mind focused on studying. It is important to understand:

The kind of person you're working with

The kind of background the individual has

The typical behaviour for a person with this type of behavior

As writers need to construct an image of their characters and characters, you're doing the same. Your first impressions may not be true However, you should take a look at the characteristics of the person and remove those characteristics from the profile. The way someone thinks is largely determined by the person they are. For instance, one might not see an individual with a wealth background thinking the same way as someone who grew up in a shabby trailer park at the middle of the wilderness. Their thinking processes will not be alike since their experiences differ greatly. Both have thoughts are able to be read, but understanding the person's thoughts is something you must master.

Patrick Jane was able to accomplish this feat. You too can accomplish this however, it will take time. Examine the subject through the eyes and then really take a look. Eyes provide a wealth of clues. If you look away, instead of looking at the image, consider, in your head about the person you see like and the feelings the person brings to your mind. It is essential to not let external influences affect your thinking. That's why the practice of meditation and other practices like this can be so beneficial. Everywhere we look there are energies, and the energy that you have to concentrate on is the one between you and the person, first through their eyes and later through an internal reflection regarding them as well as their connection to you, without having to look at them.

When you've stared them in the face and then turned away and observed how you feel about the person, you're more prone to picking the thoughts of that person.

Discussion with your subject

Begin an exchange of ideas or a dialogue to the individual whose ideas you wish to read. Then allow their thoughts to fill your thoughts. When you engage in this process you will become more compassionate and able to gain understanding of what they are really thinking. Mind reading is a process of energy flow and sharing the energy of another. If you meet the fortuneteller Do you believe that they can truly see what's happening in your head or know what the future might hold just by putting her hands in silver? The fortunetellers are able to read other people's thoughts in order to arouse the fear of people or promise them good events that will take place, but this isn't possible to do it by chance.

It's done by focusing the energy of another person, and it's proven scientifically that people can perform this, however very few spend the time to. A fortune-teller can pick up energy from their subject and has a good idea of the type of questions that will likely be asked, and gleaning responses by observing body language, signs that might be present in the subject and also in the actions and words of the person.

Additionally, psychics could convince someone that they have a connection with the deceased or even. But, the ones who can be the most convincing are those who are able to detect energy and give the person they are talking to the reassurance they require regarding a loved one who has died. Sometimes, all it takes is to assist them in moving forward in their lives. psychics who aid individuals in this way aren't to be laughed at. It's not about earning money from individuals in certain instances. There are psychics who perform their work due to the assistance they can provide.

Chapter 2: Scientists Are Saying About Mind

Reading

In the year 2005, researchers were agreeing that humans were able to read minds. In a report posted on the website Livescience.com The report revealed that empathy was the key to being capable of reading other people's minds. Human beings are able to discern the moods of other people. Although there is some debate on the nature of cognition between scientists, research in the past have demonstrated that there's a region of the brain capable of taking in thoughts of others and comprehending their thoughts.

Mirror Neurons versus Spock

The tests were conducted with a macaque monkey. The results confirmed that mirror neurons in the monkey's brain are capable of imitating or copying what the monkey observed. How does this relate to mind reading? The scientists haven't stopped there. They also discovered that mirror neurons are present in humans, however they are more mature and capable of detecting feelings and sensations, to allow a person to put themselves in the perspective of the person they're viewing and perceive things from their point of view. This is much more complex than making guesses about what an individual thinks about. It's subtle, and capable of helping people improve their relationships with each as well as of learning to demonstrate empathy in the sense that you can understand a point of perspective from another's even when words aren't spoken and the information is obtained from the emotions of the subject and the psychic.

A neuroscientist from the University of California was able to discover that rather than experiencing the same emotions as someone else individuals could actually put themselves in the mind of another person as if they were them instead of just experiencing their emotions. If this was the case the ability to read minds would be much more easy for people to attain.

The only people who seemed to be missing this particular cluster was those with autism, which means in essence, it's impossible for autistic individuals to read minds because the developed sense of mirroring is not present for them.

There is a concept known as "simulation theory" which states that people who have mirror neurons can imagine themselves in another's positions mentally, and are more attentive to what's happening in the minds of other people. Because this mirror neuron system doesn't accessible to autistic individuals They simply draw ideas about the thoughts of people through the observation.

The report discussed"Spock" theory "Spock" theory. This is an idea that doesn't rely on mirrors in the brain, but rather discovers what people think through observations. Do you recall Spock in Star Trek? One of the difficulties Spock had was empathy since there was no emotion in his body. However, his logic processes allowed him to discern what people felt or what they might be thinking, and this could be the reason why most people utilize their mind in reading, not being aware of the fact that there's more to it and once they're aware of the way mirror neurons function it is a great chance that reading the mind of another is a possibility.

Cognitive stimulation by the reading of fiction

In the year 2005 an investigation carried out by researchers from the New School for Social research produced interesting results regarding reading with the mind. The findings of the study were that people who read novels were more inclined to recognize the thoughts of others.

When asked to examine images and be able to discern emotions expressed through acting eyes readers of fiction were better at doing this. The reason for this is that geographical limitations are present because different races respond to various stimuli in different ways. Therefore those who are aware of this when they read literary reading will grow and develop the abilities needed for being able to the text on a wider size.

Human beings be affected by emotions from childhood all through their life, even though they could be restricting their geographical scope if they do not have the same emotions or feelings of those living in other parts in the globe. But, through the reading of novels set possibly in another part of the globe They are able to create an image of how people would react to specific situations in a more general way, and their pattern of cognitive precision in discerning what were going through the minds of other people would be more sophisticated.

So, this chapter offers a little background information, but it illustrates that in addition to being a host of mirror neurons, people have to recognize various methods of thinking to make use of these mirror neurons to their maximum impact. Reading fiction improves in enhancing accuracy, which means that people who read might be more receptive to emotions and emotions others are experiencing.

Exercising your psychic power

Begin to notice more than you are currently. Begin to listen more than you currently do and try to imagine yourself as they do. Try to view things from their perspective and you'll begin to look at things from a different perspective. Select your book. Make sure to change it up so that you can encounter the variety of characters you need in an environment of modern times. It is important to build this part of your brain which recognizes behaviour patterns.

Try imagining. Consider a friend as a subject . Think about how you feel regarding something that you haven't yet discussed. This could refer to something that's could take place in their life. Make them think about their thoughts on something they want to occur in the future. Concentrate on it. Take a deep dive into their thoughts by visualizing their lives in the same way they imagine it.

Before you explain to them about what you're doing, discuss other issues and try to be empathetic towards the way your friend feels. This will allow you understand the situation from their perspective. It's not easy to do it the initially, but over time, you'll realize that you are able to are able to read people more effectively than you can today. Then psychic abilities begin to begin to take over.

Things that could hinder psychic abilities

Do not assume that you know what someone else is thinking, without fully focusing on the person. If you rely on preconceived notions, you'll be unable to succeed. Mirror neurons aren't based with the basis of guesswork. They are based by observing and repetition and mirroring thoughts between psychic and subject.

Chapter 3: Empathy And The Way It Works In

Mind Reading

Everyone is constantly talking about empathy. This is the "in" term, but what exactly is it and what does it have to do with mind reading?

The real meaning to describe empathy would be:

Being capable of placing yourself in the shoes of another

Many people confuse the term "empathy" as "sympathy" and they are two distinct things. Sympathy means understanding another person's circumstances, however not always being in their position. Since you're trying to enter inside the mind of another person empathy is superior as an instrument than sympathy. In reality, sympathy can change your perception as you wish to transmit your feelings of sadness for the misfortune of someone else back to them instead of being able to take in their thoughts. You must understand how mirror neurons function to understand how sympathy can be an obstacle to being able to discern thoughts.

How do you feel empathy?

If you've been practicing the art of letting your mind go, do an hour of relaxation, whatever method you prefer to use for doing it, to ensure that you can feel compassion. You require space as the thoughts of another can take up space in your brain. You must be able to stay clear of distractions because they could distract you. Also, you must use the technique that was described in the previous chapter, looking into the eyes of a person before turning your eyes away. Why do you not look away? You have to be able to feel the emotions of your loved ones. It's not possible to do this when you keep staring at them. The reason for this is that their expression may shift between moments and can get in the way of your ability to interpret them.

There are many ways to hide things through a change in posture, which includes sending out the wrong message through their eyes. This initial interaction is sincere and will allow you to discern what they're communicating. By looking away, but listening, allows you to put you in the same position, not becoming distracted by any change in their expression. Therefore, all your attention is on your first view of their eyes, and what they say later.

How can empathy be helpful?

When you are able to feel their emotions and emotions, you can look them over, read them in the event that you want to and connect the reasoning behind the situation in relation to the message you're receiving from them. This allows you to understand what they're thinking. It allows you to spot the lies and recognize the signs that someone is being untruthful. They could be acting for some reason. If you're empathetic towards an individual, you must should take all facts into consideration and know the reasons behind them lying to you. It could be because they want to avoid harming yourself. It could also be for legitimate motives. Do not always believe that lying is a negative thing. Check out the following examples and you'll understand why.

If you ask someone how or she is doing and they respond "Fine" even though they're not. In this situation it is common to discern by their body language that something is not right, but they might be trying to avoid speaking to you due to the fact that they aren't wanting to be burdensome. This isn't an attempt to fool you. It's designed to safeguard you from having all their troubles placed upon your shoulders.

Empathy in the child

A child asks you to tell you if he's had a drink. You are sure that he has. You can smell it in his breath , and you feel that the child will not confess to it. What you aren't aware of is that the thoughts of your child could be exactly as you believe they are. He might be looking for an ways to get out of trouble, or make up a story because he is afraid you'll slip it up. Examine the body language and consider what it says about him. The reason for the lie could be that your child does not want to restrict him from being with his friends, and it is this pressure from peers that brought him into this mess in the beginning. Learn to read his thoughts. Learn to appreciate his point of view and then you'll be able to understand his thoughts.

Understanding strangers

A woman you would like to see isn't. See her with her eyes and then look away to see the reasons behind her behavior. seem insurmountable. You can look up her thoughts. It's true. Remain in the moment and take in the thoughts. The clue may be in her eyes. Turning away will cause the mirror neurons begin to activate so that you are able to feel, with empathy, what she's thinking. This is a great method to determine you should do next and can help you get out of an embarrassing circumstance.

Empathy is the feeling of taking a step into the shoes of someone else. It's about taking the issue seriously, taking it into consideration as you look at your eyes at the subject you wish to know more about, and then looking away, shutting your eyes from outside distractions and being capable of feeling their emotions and thoughts. Once you have done this it, you'll be amazed.

Training to strengthen your observation skills

It is important to practice your ability to observe as they will help you notice things you might overlook. Use a card to place a photograph on it or even the cover of a magazine that has a lot of images. Remain in a comfortable posture and stare intently over the image. Be sure to take in every information and, when you think you've got everything in your head take the card off or turn the page in the magazine to make sure you don't observe it. Then, write down the exact details of the details you observed. This isn't just a simple memory exercise. This is an exercise designed to improve your observation skills. Some characters like Patrick Jane did this in the TV show , but they did it with an objective. They could discern things that others thought were insignificant. It also allowed them to discern certain aspects about someone which others wouldn't be able to discern.

The aim is to improve the skills you have and refine the skills. Utilize observation in public areas and take note of the details of each person not only the initial thoughts of what they look like. You must learn to read people involves seeing at things beyond what is visible. It's about noticing things others do not see. Is your subject nervous? Take a look at their fingernails, as this will give you lots of details. Are they infected? Are they properly cared for? Do they have a bad reputation? There are a lot of clues available, but all you have to do is look for clues instead of making a decision using guesswork.

Chapter 4: People Who Naturally Read Minds

Have you ever met couples who are so close, that one is capable of finishing the sentences of the other? It's not uncommon, but it requires an extremely well-informed couple to achieve it. What they are doing when they complete the sentence of their companion is mind-reading. They are aware of what is about to happen. They know that the person speaking will be slow in saying it , and they are able to finish with the sentence.

This same type of mind reading can be utilized by people who have a common situation, an aspect of solidarity or have a common backgrounds, however it may go beyond the above. When you are able to read the scientific aspects is a good start. The greater the scope of your knowledge of reactions and emotions to stimuli, the more skilled of reading minds.

It is also important to brush the body language as there are times when people can be accused of displaying a fake smile. Therefore, they cover their emotions in a deliberate manner. If someone has even thought for a moment that you were able to understand their thoughts, problems arise. Not only do the thoughts change rapidly and people also play games and discuss obscure issues to keep from being able to read their true thoughts. So, those who possess the capacity to discern thoughts, don't use it to play games. They must acknowledge to recognize that this is a gift and that they do have it because they are educated about:

Emotional reactions

Physical reactions

Body language

Three major elements that are used to guide your mind when you read. Mind reading isn't a sport. It's not about somebody thinking of a play card, and then trying to figure out the meaning of the playing card. It's more complex than this. It's about learning to enter into the mind of another person and look at what's happening in their head. It's an effective aid to others and for understanding the emotional challenges that individuals face.

It's also very helpful for understanding the reality of an issue. It's difficult to conceal your truth to someone else who is able to detect your thoughts and imagine themselves in your shoes . It's something that everyone can master, with the exception of autistic people However, it's not something that many are aware of anyhow because they're too distracted by their own issues or the demands of their lives, or the whirlwind of their thoughts.

People with the aptitude to understand their partner's words after many years of marriage possess that empathy. They know what their spouse will say. They are aware of what they're thinking about since they practice their art each all day. The energy and the aura that they share are often coupled, and so knowing the thoughts of the partner is a natural thing to do. After years of living with each other, it's an automatic thing for them to have the same thoughts which makes mind reading easier than it would be for other people.

With experience and a greater feeling of empathy, it is possible to attain that level of empathy with a stranger. It's just a matter of the time to practice. Consider other relationships in which the same oneness can be felt. Two close friends may be a part of this same feeling as individuals who spend their entire lives together. The common background of these friends allows them to slip into and out of one another's shoes, and be able to read each other's thoughts. Imagine unity. It's essential to understand minds. If you are able to observe their emotions as you absorb their personality and this is how they think.

Oneness is the key to understanding another person's thoughts.

Chapter 5: Tips From Professional Mind Readers

Mind readers with experience who play in their mind-reading skills in front of strangers are conscientious about their selection of topics. Mentalist Gerry McCambridge, in an interview with the Daily Explainer told readers about the way he makes use of certain emotions to gather information about the subject matter in his readings of the mind. Visitors flock to his shows because they know that they'll receive an excellent value, however this value comes from a heightened feeling of being able to make use of the mirror neurons that we spoke about earlier. Even though McCambridge does not mention these in any scientific fashion however, he does state the use of mirroring techniques that are quite similar.

It is important to remember that you're trying to replicate the thoughts of another. In response to questions about what type of subject he picks from the crowd, McCambridge was very specific. He doesn't pick the person who is a showman and wants 5 minutes fame because that's the intelligent Alec who thinks "outside out of the box" deliberately. He selects someone less likely to accept his invitation however, he chooses someone with the confidence to step up on the stage.

Look for people who are sympathetic.

When he looks around the audience in the course of an event, he is looking at people that are similar wavelength as he is. It is possible to determine this by watching who is laughing at which jokes or who's facial expressions indicate that they're captivated by the same kind of thoughts that he is. He utilizes Neuro Linguistic Programming for the purpose of analyzing the thoughts that people have in their minds. This method is utilized by many people to free their minds. If you believe that you are gifted and you would like to be able to read minds, it's good to consider taking the course to learn about Neuro Linguistic Programming as it will prepare you to interact with any person and be open-minded in the way you interact with strangers.

Helping your subject feel comfortable

After deciding on the person to be his candidate, he helps them feel comfortable by speaking to them and listening attentively to their responses, and then mirroring them back to the person in order to be completely connected to the person. The way they interact with each other is an important aspect of the mind's ability to read. For instance, McCambridge makes sense when the author states that you can't expect a positive response in the event that you are not on the same wavelength as the subject.

If the person you are talking to is retiring and shy and retiring, then speaking to them in a calm and retiring way will make them feel more comfortable than speaking to them with a loud voice or rude tone. In real life it is a skill that you must master for if you want to be able to read minds.

McCambridge has been on so many of these shows that he is able to predict responses pretty accurately and analyzes the type of people who will be arriving to the show, so that he can provide additional statistics for things like the type of vehicles they own as well as whether they're having an extended wait before getting in the show, and how open they're likely to be, and so on. A few interesting techniques McCambridge explains to viewers is that there are predetermined responses that he can be fairly precise with.

Utilizing statistical data

If, for instance, one asked someone in a quick choice method to decide on an appropriate color, red is the most likely option. Quick answers are usually different from thoughtful responses. Selecting a number that is between 1 and 10 is likely to result in, in 90% of percent of cases, the results of the number chosen 7. When it comes to color the thing he observes is that when people have more time they will generally consider "Oh sure, I'll pick red, because it's obvious" and choose the other option, that is blue.

A clever trick that you should play with someone who is interested in reading minds to have enjoyment. You can tell your subject to respond "no" to anything you inquire about. After that, prompt your subject to come up with an amount that is between one to 10. You can follow that by asking, "Is the number 1?" And go through the numbers. In the course in the game if you've asked the players to say "no" to each and every question, they will be able be lying to you. You can spot the lying. See if there is the change in their posture. See if their eyes are towards the downwards. There are clues present and can be used to determine what's going on in the mind of a person.

There's a trick the magician uses that is like the tricks employed to trick Patrick Jane in The Mentalist. If you are able to hold the arm of someone as you ask them a question, you'll be able to feel the that the muscles shift when a lie is presented and thus are in a position to discern the truth from the fiction and understand what's going on in the brain of your person you are talking to. It's extremely beneficial and often people don't even notice the warmth that is an natural flow of the conversation. There are a variety of indicators to look out for when you're a reader, you must be aware of the signs. Does your person look after themselves? This will tell you lots about confidence and concerns with self-esteem. Does your subject lie? There are many various body language signs which will let you know when the person you are talking to is lying. Watch for a blink in the eyes. Also, look for those who stare downwards when they provide an answer. You can see the flickering of fingers.

Patrick Jane didn't just take into consideration the appearance of the subject. He was observant of the surrounding and also because he wanted to understand the entire pictureinstead of making the assumption. If you want to make people open to conversation, you must be friendly. If you begin conversations in the same serene manner, you will promote open dialogue. If you begin the conversation by making accusations, the reactions of people alter and it's not as easy to understand them.

But, if you can determine what the typical response of a person to a query that isn't quite expected and you are able to get them to slack off by their body language as they are caught off guard. Patrick Jane does this a frequently, using words that are completely unsuitable to gain information. People who are insecure and have something to hide can't be uncovered without clever methods. You need be on guard whenever Patrick Jane is in action because his character is extremely cleverly based on the concept of psychic abilities employed for deceit and trickery however, it is also well-developed to make use of it for good. Patrick Jane started as a con artist, but later he used his observation skills that he never considered psychic abilities to assist police in solving crimes.

The most important thing to remember in this book is observe. This assists the psychic or person trying to improve their psychic abilities to gain the upper hand and discern people more precisely. The process of observation is in sync with positive interactions. This technique is utilized worldwide by psychics to understand the information that their clients are amazed to know. All of this can be obtained from precise observation and catching people off from being on.

Chapter 6: Activities To Enhance Your Mind-

Reading Skills

There are many other things you can try to boost your clairvoyance abilities. Some might seem odd but they're not unreasonable and do work by opening your mind to new ideas that you may not be presently open to. For instance, reading someone from another culture could be challenging because the symbols and signs you receive are different from those you're used to. One way to deal with this is to employ these tools in expanding your mind.

Reading

The ability to read across all genres of literature can help you absorb the vast array of information. From reading fiction to factual reading, it provides you with an expanded vocabulary. It can help you understand the different cultures and kinds of characters. For instance, if were American you would think that American subjects to hold standards and concepts which are similar to those you were taught. But, reading can open up an entire world of people and how they respond. International clairvoyants will therefore be able to better understand characters and how they behave in situation. This can help them in their reading of individuals because it cuts away the boundaries. If you plan to start reading to learn how to understand characters in a more efficient way, choose authors are known to be excellent character profilers.

Expand your reading to ensure that it includes the type of people that you do not get daily in contact with. Every character type is great learning tools which includes those suffering from mental illness or who are prone to psychopathic traits. The more you learn about the human mind, the better in identifying it and reading the signs. Doctors often can tell by the look of a patient if they will react positively to an alternative. This is because they meet patients every day and are aware of the attitude of patients who come to them to get reassurance, not being in need of medical treatment. It is essential that they do the Job done right. Since there isn't a whole number of stories about medical errors and placebos aren't causing any harm to the body It's possible that this practice is utilized more frequently than you thought.

Practicing

This can be very helpful. Ask your friends to assist If you'd like, and make sure to demonstrate to them how you can see what is in their heads. If you ask them to do this immediately, they'll come up with obscure ideas since they aren't comfortable with the thought that their minds could be being read. But, if you wait until there are gaps during the discussion, you could be able to observe the conversation and may be able to second the idea of what they're about to or say. This makes them easily clairvoyant subjects. If the answer of someone is obvious, then clairvoyants have to ask the correct questions. If you make a connection with the subjects that matter for the person you are trying to understand and you can see immediate changes in their attitude. When you touch something sensitive and they will get up, so you'll be able to discern right immediately what areas to look into that are causing them trouble.

The idea is that a skilled discerner can use his or her talents to aid others. It is not a skill to be utilized for negative purposes. The energy that is generated by thoughts is positive in its energy that you can detect this and come up with very insightful answers to questions from someone regarding their future, about their love life , their health issues and even about the family cat when you recognize the messages they give off.

The ability to read someone else's thoughts can be useful to you as a psychic as it grants you the ability to assist. If you observe that someone is crying and you want to know why they feel this way is useful. You should find the reason why people are clammy and why they are afraid or anxieties and then discover how you can provide them with the answers they're seeking. Many people seeking the assistance of a psychic are doing so due to a lack of confidence in their ability to accomplish their goals. However, this is not true as everyone can work toward a target. If your clairvoyant sessions is to assist someone in their everyday routine or see their possible in the near future, suggestions are very effective.

You'll have a happy marriage. Sure you will. You believe in what the clairvoyant stated because it is in line to your beliefs and increases your confidence to bring the marriage to be in a state in which it is secure and content.

There will be the Prince charming. Okay, this is somewhat silly, but if a person thinks they'll see similar events happen in their life and it does, then it will happen. It is not really predicting the future. What you're doing is analyzing the type of person you choose as a subject, figuring the goals they're aiming for, and the next step is to assure them that things are going to happen that they strive to achieve since you predicted that it could occur. So, when you do get it your reputation improves and people spread the word to others the fact that you could aid them.

Chapter 7: Preparing To Give Readings

In Victorian times , there an abundance of faith in clairvoyant readings. They were not solely for fun. Did these readings have more meaning as they do now? No, certainly they didn't. If someone is looking for the assistance of psychics the reason is that they are unable to see the future they would like to, and believe that your vision of their future is more accurate than yours. They're usually right, as many people seek this type of therapy often to provide an affirmation or suggestion.

The stage is set for the beginning of a story

If you invite someone to the tent, with an outdoor table covered in an apron and place at the table a basic crystal ball, it's hard to claim to be being a psychic. These are circus acts , and this is how it will be seen. Therefore, it is essential to create a space where you can see your clients professionally set up. You require a comfortable chair for them to provide them with peace of mind. You require bookcases that house numerous books that are scholarly because they get an impression that you're educated and know what you're talking about. Tables are always a good prop, and the smell of incense or a pleasant scent can enhance the ambience greatly.

Keep in mind that they are seeking help because they aren't convinced about themselves or their ability to communicate about the past or locate their way into the future. Can we speak to dead people? Yes, they are able to and many simply have to do it in order in order to come to a conclusion. It's not likely that the dead would rise up and speak to them, although some clairvoyants are in a position to sense energies that take forms of messages. For instance, if you notice a warm glow and warmth, you can tell it's positive one. If you feel cold and feel a chill, then the message will not seem as positive. But, establishing the scene in a way that is credible and trustworthy is essential.

Your approach to customers

This is pretty common practice. If the dentist greets patients with an instrument in his hand is likely to terrorize an individual into submission, but the dentist will not make him feel comfortable and open. An appointment with a clairvoyant can be an interaction and it is essential that the person seeking assistance receives a warm welcome and compassion and given the impression that his or her voice is heard. The person who clairvoyants work with will more than just listen. A good clairvoyant will be capable of recognizing the nature of their subject and their demands because it's their job to fulfill those requirements. It's also a two-way relationship and you must be clear with the client before you begin the session. The two of you work on their issues in tandem. The problem isn't just coming from you. This means they are more open to discussion and gives you the opportunity to hear their issues and empathize with them. Keep in mind that empathy is about placing yourself in their shoes and viewing the issue from the point from which they view it.

Understanding the needs of others

They are available in many forms, but if one tries to figure out the common sense explanation the client is calling your computer, your sense will recognize the facets of the reason. For instance, they may be calling to discuss one of the following:

* Love

* Work

* Career

* Health

* Emotions

* Relationships with people

* Dreams and aspirations

* Unrequited love

There are many reasons one might want to consult the professional clairvoyant. Famous people like Princess Diana was a clairvoyant who was helped by her during her life. Sally Morgan also astounded Australian presenters on TV when she predicted the events that could happen to presenters. The predictions proved to be the case. How? It is possible to conclude that she had psychic abilities or think that she was a wise person. Whichever one you pick to believe is irrelevant because her predictions were accurate. Understanding a bit about your subject is crucial to succeed because what you see can be influenced by how you feel. This is crucial for psychic readers.

Let's see if we can show you how to do this:

You've spoken via the phone to an interested client who has stated that she would like to have another child and that it is important to her more than any other thing on earth. Then, you notice certain vibrations and you realize that there's something wrong but don't know what's wrong until you see her. You make lots of work prior to the appointment, but when you walk in and you discover that the woman has passed the age of childbearing, it is believed been interpreted as a sign that there are different areas of her life creating problems for her. The process of aging could be adroitly identified as the thing she is most afraid of which is why she will hide in the guise of wanting to have another child.

What happens is that it's impossible to determine the cause of the issue or visit without actually getting to know the person. If you bring both of these elements together, you can get an improved understanding of the complete picture is and this is so vital. In the case of Diana it's clear that a celebrity such as her required lots of comfort because of the personal issues she faced. Since the psychic was already aware of the issue and knew exactly the issues and what was causing them, it was much easier for her to see what the future would bring.

Props required

If you can identify the kind of problem that someone is facing by talking about them prior to an appointment and the issue is related to another person who died or passed away, it could be beneficial to keep an object that belonged to the deceased since the energy of this object might provide clues to the psychic to find answers. This item will be valuable to the person who is seeking it and must be handled with care. Other items that are useful to keep in your possession are charts to aid the interpretation of hand in order to be able to explain and support the information you're giving the client using the chart. If a psychic or clairvoyant uses astronomy in their readings, then charts can assist because the client is required to enter specific details about their personal information like time and date of birth. You will also have to match these details to the problems the person is experiencing.

Clairvoyants' props as well as psychics are generally those that aid in proving the things they're doing, so that the person receiving the information can be more certain in what they're being presented with and what it's based upon. We've progressed a lot from the Victorian times when clairvoyants intimidated people with stories that could frighten people into believing certain things concerning their own lives. In the present day people are increasingly questioning about their methods, and having information that can answer their questions can help them increase their trust in the system that is in use.

Chapter 8: Readings

It is always beneficial for psychics to meet with potential clients in a relaxed setting prior to making appointments. It could be an introduction session which allows the psychic to examine the person, and gives them the opportunity to explain the methods they employ. This can help the client feel comfortable when they arrive for their reading as they already know the procedure which will be used and are more comfortable with the psychic as they've met them before.

Mirror Techniques

They are used already in psychology to aid individuals recognize their own issues. Psychologists can mirror what that the client is saying to the person who is listening to them, so that they can listen to the issue and seeing the issue from a different perspective. It's highly efficient and has been proved to be effective. In the earlier chapters of the book, we spoke about mirror neurons and we also talked about empathy as the key that can be used to activate the mirror neurons, and thus being able see problems from the viewpoint of the person who is suffering instead of acting as an observer.

Mirror techniques are a way of taking in what the subject is experiencing. It is a step above empathy because instead of just thinking about what they feel the psychic is actually feeling the suffering and anger, is able to feel the anger and the disappointment of the person who they are treating. It helps psychics since they're no longer viewing at the world from afar. They're actually looking at their thought process from inside.

Mirror techniques can also be employed to gather more data. The psychic who is listening to someone but not able to see the whole picture can make use of generalizations that help the person in need to discuss about their real issues. The phrases that pop into your head are easy ones like:

* Does this seem logical to you?

* I'm trying to understand the concept of

* What is the reason you believe that?

* What connections does this have to your daily life?

They're generalizations, however they have a reason which is to assist in extracting more information, so that psychics are able to recognize the energy and see a more clear image so that they can move from being a spectator to actually being in the mind of the subject, and view the situation from an empathic perspective. This can be very helpful in readings that are connected to the individual's experiences that they aid the patient work towards higher-quality goals.

A suggested reading prior to psychic readings to help to ensure accurate readings.

Science cannot be ruled out of the facts. In a certain degree, the the psychological reaction to stimuli will determine the outcome. The most beneficial books for psychics to study are those that help open ways to greater understanding. Gail Sheehy wrote an extremely excellent book that I have to use as a reference.

I read again and repeatedly because it's such a great information. This book came out nearly 30 years ago. It's known as Passages and is definitely an interesting read prior to the session with the client.

Tuning to the tune set by the client

It is crucial for success. If you could have 10 readings with a specific client, there is a chance that some of your predictions might not happen. But, if you inform your client what they want to hear move forward in their lives believing that something might happen, and their outlook changes to the problem. For instance, it's unlikely that Diana would have wanted to hear that. Diana would have liked to be told that she would lose her life in an automobile crash but it might have made her more wary to never get in another car! She needed the strength of her emotions and her psychic helped her achieve this. Most people want an option to move forward, and psychics are excellent in this regard. You wouldn't advise men to divorce their wife. You might suggest that there are changes in the works and he'll make the decision on his own since it's been coming up for many years. You will be praised for telling him something that profoundly altered his life. In the end the only thing you did was recommend that he make a change. The rest was up to him.

Don't make promises with a certain nature that can't be fulfilled. You might think that this is something that isn't quite right in a particular instance, but with a psychic I had known, she claimed to have told her client she would be blessed with twins. It was also unlikely since the husband had had an operation called a vasectomy, but also because the woman had no chance of having twins since she had never been unfaithful to her spouse and her husband was unable to provide her with children. This was a odd situation because this reading led the lady to look for love elsewhere, and her life was taken in completely different directions. She believed she was going to have twins , but knew her husband was not capable of having twins. There was a twist to the story when the man was able to meet and marrled a younger lady and had the vasectomy reversed. Did he get twins? Actually, he did. The reason for this is that if you're too naive in your assessment of situations , you may make mistakes that can affect the lives of people.

Instead of telling the woman she was about have twins could be more precise by providing a less intrusive explanation like:

"Do twins form part of the family?"

If the woman's response was to the contrary, there could have been subtle hint. If the man was able to produce twins in a second woman, she may be thinking of how clever the psychic was, rather than feeling angry because she assumed that the twins were likely become hers.

The hints in the form of a veiled veil, or small things that come to mind aid the psychic in digging into the dirt. Here are a few words that can help you understand what is meant by this:

"I see the initial letter A" It's a common scenario because people will instantly react. What person doesn't have the first letter A?

"I see red" In reality, it could be any color you want and you can quite accurately look at colors that match individuals and provide an exact representation.

"I believe that good things are in the near future" What exactly does this mean? It's another somewhat vague, but extremely positive declaration. It could be money or be another kind of luck.

"I am receiving a message" ..."" - This could be used in a séance in which a psychic seeks to contact the dead. It also offers amazing clues. Anyone who is waiting for the message will be bursting with enthusiasm and will usually reveal clues while doing so.

Chapter 9: Responsibilities That Are Part Of

Being A Psychic

It's an excellent idea to be aware that you are accountable to the people around you for the consequences that could occur due to your forecasts or the statements you make to people. There are moral issues that you must not touch with regard to because, if you do not then you could ruin your reputation and harm the reputation of those who are psychics and utilize their psychic abilities to assist others. It's a problem that it is a grey subject and since there is no set of rules that people who are reckless and are experimenting in Psychic readings or reading minds often create damage more than they do good in some instances.

Let me give you an example or two to ensure that you can identify areas you shouldn't touch or make a decision about.

If you're visited by someone who appears mentally unstable due to her circumstance. At first glance that she's anxious; she may be experiencing depression, and it comes to the forefront in a manner that can affect her self-esteem. The goal of psychic readings is not to provide her with false hope, but rather the human reaction is to soothe and assure her that everything is going to be alright. The problem is that empathy is not utilized. It is important to remember that empathy involves being in her position. You cannot accomplish this without some sort of concept of the situation from the perspective of a realist and what she is telling you isn't real. It could be based on what she believes based on her current state of mind. If you are using empathy, you aren't going far off the mark because all the warning signs are present If you do invite her to get her former abusive partner back, or maybe convince her that the person who abandoned her will return What you are doing is allow levels of false hopes that could push her over the edge. It's not ethical, isn't based on empathy and does not help anyone, not especially her.

The type of optimism you could offer in a situation like this is, again, a little ambiguous however it could be optimistic. It is the idea to utilize your psychic abilities to make her feel more positive about her circumstances. Examples of phrases include:

* I see good developments on the horizon

* I can see your life situation getting better

These phrases offer her positive feedback that doesn't have to rely on her partner coming again. It is possible to even amp these to a certain extent by giving subtle clues, but don't make false claims that your partner will come back as it could end in more than tears.

Are psychic abilities available to anyone?

They can, but they do not actually achieve a credible quality of psychic abilities due to the fact that they're not able to comprehend and use their abilities for good motives. If you view psychic abilities as something that you can make lots of money off of and you think that it is, then you're in the wrong field because the main goal of psychics is to utilize their abilities for serve the greater good and assist others. If you are in the mindset that you are looking to exploit people to make money or money, then you're not the best person to do such a position. Let those who are. You can begin looking in different directions or become more helpful to those around you until you can pursue it with the good motives.

Are psychics obligated to report wrongdoings law?

It's a question mark due to it is possible that something was confessed by psychics that involved a person in the commission of a crime. If someone was accused of murdering someone else and wanted to communicate with the soul of the person in order to resolve the matter. In the world of medicine there are laws in place to stop confidential information from being divulged however, what does it mean to be psychic? I have actually come across this and realized that psychics do not enjoy the same confidentiality rules as doctors have. Therefore, if you discover that someone is responsible for a crime then the best course of action is to behave in a professional manner till the interview is completed and then report anyone you suspect is at risk due to themselves as well as their actions or from any other person who could be at risk due to your subject's interaction with them.

Many psychics collaborate in conjunction with Law Enforcement agencies to help solve crimes. However, they are usually psychics with a demonstrated experience of accomplishment in a specific area. These psychics can be employed to identify the body of a person, or assist the police with the investigation of particular crimes that are difficult to solve within their competence.

Chapter 10: Learning Your Psychic Powers

There are several things you can try to boost your observation skills and ability to discern. For instance, ask your friends to assist you to have enjoyment. Bring them cards and request for them to pick one. Make them concentrate for as long as they can on that card, and then sit on the opposite end of the table trying to determine if the card is red or black and what kind of suit it belongs to, if the card is low or high in the pack and then finally knowing what the card's identity is. Do this without them noticing that you're asking them anything other than vague questions. It is possible to employ tricks employed by magicians to divert the focus off of the task at hand.

Mirrors as Neurons during exercises

The memory game from an earlier chapter is vital for those looking to build psychic abilities. Go into an area and try to gather all the information is possible regarding the area you're in. You must then answer the questions below correctly and check your answers against the facts.

• How many chairs were available inside the conference room?

* What was the color of the carpet? Were there any other rugs?

* What artifacts were there in the first place? And where did it get hung?

The main focus in the space?

* What number of doors did the room contain?

What was the color of paintwork used on the doors?

The room have wallpaper?

Which color did the ceiling have?

* Did a light fixture on the ceiling or other types of lamps light up the space?

* What color was the lampshades?

The ability to observe is essential for the psychic and mind reader. A skilled psychic is able to see things in their surroundings that other people don't. If you are able to practice these abilities often to improve your understanding or ability to visualize. You are able to go back to that room at whenever you'd like to, if you walk into the room for at first with an open head and a picture in your mind , and ask yourself questions. If you walk into to the space with filled mind, you'll see little or no details. Mirror neurons aren't able to be activated because there is too much happening between them and the capacity to focus.

Feeling empathy

In this exercise, which you need to be practicing regularly, get your friends involved and solicit their assistance. Tell them some of their experiences and try to get into their thoughts and observe how adept you are at empathizing. Be aware that this isn't about giving suggestions from the outside. It's about entering their heads in order to an examination of problems in the same way they do.

Ask your friends to join in a psychic séance and only ask questions that are veiled or declarations. Do not ask direct questions.

asked. The reason for this is to test how adept you are at predicting their mental state. Imagine that you are your friend's client, and the client is seeking an appointment with a psychic. Bring your friend into the room, and ensure that the person you are inviting is at ease.

Did you remember how we suggested you should look at your client and offer every positive suggestion and then turn away? Do it because it's an excellent strategy particularly if you managed to find a bit of practice time before getting participants. Try to get used to a chattering line that doesn't blur your vision but lets you listen to the voices of your friends and listen to what they're talking about. You can make use of things like needing to enter a stupor to show that you're not paying attention to them. It is also possible to determine the emotional state of them through their words or utter or the words they use and words that are not said. Make use of all your abilities to leap from your own mind to theirs.

This helps you improve your skills. Do you remember the way horoscopes are published in newspapers or magazines? They make vague suggestions instead of making specific statements, because it's impossible to say for sure that every Capricorn on earth will feel sick on a certain day. This isn't logical. Instead, they employ terms like "off forms" or "watch for indicators of health problems." It's the same thing mediums say. They don't inform a patient that they will cause the client suffer from cancer or make any particular claim. They are prone to using vague words to create a suggestion, and the suggestion could work with the people's lives. This is something you should be able to do. This isn't a form of trickery. It's just clever manipulation of circumstances to ensure you're in control.

Exercise on generalizations

In this practice it is a simple matter of examining how you interact with others without divulging too much about you. As psychic, it's about them, not you. You have to be able and able to steer the conversation in a way that what you say and do is react to what the customer indicates to be the cause of their issue. Discuss problems with people. These could be relatives, friends, or anyone you know but you need to be sure to listen. What you do as you listen is to become accustomed to the kinds of things people complain about , and also determine where these negative thoughts come from.

Do this with every person you meet. Utilize autosuggestion as it is frequently used by psychologists, and it can be used by psychics and mediums. When you receive a message that is negative, transform it into the form of a question. A good example is provided below. This can reveal more than what the reader believes they are and this is beneficial for psychics.

Client: I'm having a bad day today (expecting the sympathy of).

The psychic: We must determine the reason for experiencing a lack of energy. It's typically a matter of examining the areas of your life, and then determining what your future holds.

Client: I've experienced many issues working with my colleagues. I'm not getting along with everyone well.

Psychological: So you've been having this issue with colleagues. Are you saying you believe this is the reason you're feeling unwell?

What you're doing is using mirroring strategies without saying anything at all. The mirrors are letting them do the talking. Have a few conversations similar to that. And within the following chapter we will discuss the useful art of being able utilize suggestion to obtain results. The suggestion of psychics or people who has psychic abilities, is very effective indeed.

Chapter 11: Using Suggestion

It's funny, but I have a good friend who is quite pale, and while she was in vacation, her time was destroyed because everyone kept saying that she was sick. The effect of suggestion is effective and psychics utilize often to help their clients reach the best possible state of mind throughout their lives. Princess Diana often went to a psychic as she needed some assurance. In a time when life was spiraling out of control she was able to focus and it greatly helped her. Numerous famous people have used psychics in a similar method.

If you take a look at the list of famous people who have used psychics, you might be amazed to learn that US Presidents have used them frequently. It is remarkable and comprises John F. Kennedy, Bill Clinton, Teddy Roosevelt, Woodrow Wilson, Herbert Hoover and many others. It might seem odd to those who don't understand how psychics operate, but every one of them had the confidence of governing their country. They were obviously concerned about the results of their choices, and psychics would not make those choices for them. What they could do was listen and make suggestions and their suggestions are potent indeed.

Take a look at the celeb aspect of the picture and you will see celebrities you admire like Brad Pitt, Patrick Swayze and Cameron Diaz consult with their psychics frequently. What is it that draws people to a psychic? If you can answer the question to this question, you have a fantastic tip to use to treat clients, and how your suggestions can go far in giving the client a sense of security. You might be wondering what type of assurance an attractive person such as Brad Pitt would want but the fame of Brad Pitt doesn't come with the assurance of happiness. Patrick Swayze sees his psychic as a way to prove that his psychic helped him put his marriage back in order and it's a difficult task for someone who are at this level to accomplish.

While none of these psychics talk about their interactions with their top clients, there is one thing that is for certain. They would've felt with the client. They will be in the position of the person they were talking to and be able to understand the fears which the person was facing. For instance, who tells the star what role they should play? Imagine this. A star in the spotlight is concerned about being cast in a controversial movie because they aren't certain what the film will mean for their future. A psychic who can pick the actor's personal feelings for the role can alter his entire life by its power. will only require extremely simple and vague claims in order to accomplish this.

This is an effort to positive move.

* It seems like you're feeling positive about this film role

It doesn't sound anything like Brad Pitt. Brad Pitt that the public are familiar with.

Okay, so the final suggestion wasn't based on reality, but imagine receiving a message similar to that of psychic. It's likely to play played a role in the decision of Brad Pitt wanted to change his image or prefers to keep his status. The final decision must always be left to the individual

However, suggestions could affect his decision in either way or the other. It's an extremely significant thing as it alters lives. This also means that should Brad Pitt was to believe that the role that was offered to him could make him appear to be someone different from the norm He would need to consider the risks on his own and make an informed decision based on his own beliefs. The suggestion is the one used to direct the direction. The client is able to make their own choices.

There are some psychics who give people exact numbers of children they'll have. However, it's a risky way to go since there are many reasons for why these predictions might not come true. There are however suggestions that are based on empathy, such as:

* I have the impression that you'd be an excellent material for parents.

* I'm getting the feeling that your child will play a role in your life.

Both can be identified through feelings of empathy, however, the individual isn't being informed that she'll have the joy of having a child. The woman is being careful to be guided toward becoming a mother. even if health issues get impeding her or if her relationship ends it's not going to stop her from adopting. The second suggestion is actually an excellent suggestion. It follows the safer route that could result in the mother deciding to adopt and be grateful to her psychic has brought it issue to her focus.

As you can see, that this suggestion actually provided to the person a way to move into. A psychic can be an advisor and some psychics today serve as mentors or anyone who is able to give solid, reliable guidance. What they do is go inside the mind of a person and feel their emotions and make suggestions that are sensible and logical in their approach to what they perceive the person is feeling.

Chapter 12: Communicating With The Dead

There are many states that allow a medium to communicate with spirits. However, you can master it on your own. Communication occurs during a time when the mind has entered a state of mind that is known as the hypnagogic state. It's possible that you don't realize it, however everyone has the capability communication with the spirits however the majority of people do not use this in their daily lives. Instead, they opt for mediums to feel they're receiving professional assistance, which makes the process much easier. If you're summoning spirits that are dead, be aware that the person who wishes to speak to you will give you lots of clues, however they'll want to see their worth. They'll want proof to prove that you really did connect with spirits and will require you to comprehend the procedure.

There is a possibility that you have heard of Lucid Dreaming. It is as well in this state. It is the state that you attain at the moment you are about to go to sleep. Your mind could be wandering, you might visualize images in your head or even hear noises. Some even hear voices. But the point is that it's difficult to pinpoint who it is you're seeking without some kind of thought in your head. Affixing something that belonged to the deceased may help.

The first thing you should understand is why the customer is interested in keeping in contact with the deceased. Maybe they'd like to be acknowledged or perhaps they never had the chance to express their gratitude. Maybe it's just as easy as wanting closure. Sometimes, however it's more complicated than that, and the customer requires specific answers to certain questions , and they're not necessarily easy to identify.

Researchers have examined this time in time and have found that the activity of the brain is extremely active in fact. In reality both theta as well as Alpha brain waves can be in full swing during this state. It is recommended to seek professional assistance to attain the state you desire, or you might have enough experience with hypnagogic states that you can achieve it during your relaxation sessions. If so lucky enough to be there, then you're very lucky as you can utilize it to help you focus on the energy you want to attain.

The absence of beta activity signifies that normal mind patterns can be slow, and it suggests that everyday problems individuals are typically focused on actually decrease during this phase of sleep. This is possible by training your brain to shut off through relaxation or by entering into an euphoria. Mediums and psychics are trained to enter the state of trance in order that they can utilize this technique to assist their clients communicate with dead people However, it's crucial to determine what the person wants to accomplish since this will aid you to find this particular spirit as well as answers to their questions.

If you're not able to attain trance state by yourself, it doesn't mean you can't achieve it. It is possible that you require training to be able to do this. There are many excellent videos on YouTube by professionals that can assist you in your learning. The only thing you must keep in mind is that you provide your customer no assurance that you'll be able to keep contact with their loved ones, but you're willing to give it a shot.

There are a few minor variations that could be noticed in the course of a conversation. The client will likely test you to determine if the individual whom you're talking to is in fact their relatives. They may want an exact description of the person and it's not completely off the mark to claim that spirits aren't always considered to be human. Other possibilities may arise when you look at things as images of uniformity or similar thoughts in a pictures in your mind. Sometimes, they are compatible and other times they do not.

If you're interested in developing your abilities as a psychic, it's recommended to continue studying this by enrolling in a class on how to harness your psychic abilities to attain this state of mind , and utilize it to connect with the dead since most people seek that comfort. If you decide to take the test, do not try to fake it. It's not worth the reputation you have earned although certain "psychics" have a reputation for it. They might not do much harm, and may offer reassurance of loved ones who are gone however they're not helping the credibility of genuine psychics in doing this.

Patrick Jane used suggestion and even veiled remarks to show that he was able to discern messages from spirits, but the methods he employed were observation and an extremely clever method of listening to the minds of people to find clues and using these clues to be in line with what the client wants to hear. In a way , this can be beneficial to the client and can help them put ghosts to rest and let them go to sleep however, it's not the best approach to handle requests to be put into contact with the spirits of deceased loved ones. This is a highly specialization and even if you aren't experiencing it yourself, when you approach that point before bed it is possible that training can help you attain that level of expertise , so that you can assist clients in their need.

Chapter 13: Support For Mind Readers

If you think you're destined to this type of work or have had the experience of being able to predict the future with accuracy that is efficient, it could be worth contacting with a professional group which can assist you in learning to improve your abilities. Many people who are gifted with psychic abilities don't realize until much later that they are gifted. They think they can see the world the same way as others do until they experience something that it shows them that they aren't just speculation. If you are in this very small percentage of people with an unnatural talent, take meticulous notes of your accomplishments and what you have accomplished in your life to ensure that experts can look at your talents and determine if they can enhance them.

If you truly believe you've got a talent There's a fantastic site that will test your talents and it also offers you experts to call to get your abilities evaluated in a real-time situation. Input this address into your browser and you'll be given a variety of tests designed to assist you in determining your strengths, and weak points.

What I liked most about this website is the way the tests are broken down into various categories. Tests can be taken for various things like Tarot Reading ability, Zener cards, readings based on pictures as well as telekinesis and ESP tests. Random number tests and the letter tests are enjoyable and you can take these tests at home, if you'd like to. I performed them using playing cards, and Lexicon cards with the letters on them, laying them towards the downwards on the table, and then trying to determine the letter by putting all my attention to the cards, and waiting for the energy to return to me with a message telling me what the card contained.

It took some time to get more outcomes, however I succeeded since psychic powers are similar to other abilities. You can improve in it, and it's worth it to develop. There are certain things I've realized that I'm not skilled at. For instance psychics I have personally met who can summon spirits. I am impressed of their ability. When I communicate with spirits, it's a issue of fragmented images or sounds. It is pretty amazing to be in the same room with spirits as my friends from the field have informed me that they have.

When you begin to develop your psychic abilities as well as the capacity to discern minds, or the use of ESP You may find this site entertaining, however, you could also find it useful to discover others who have tales to tell and whose experiences could provide clues to how you can enhance your abilities.

It is possible that the James Randi Education Foundation may be also looking for your abilities as psychics. They has thrown out the gauntlet through the Million Dollar Challenge and it's worth noting in a book relating to the supernatural as well as the ways psychics can be able to prove their claims. If you prove to be extremely talented, you may have the chance of winning however, you must be ready because the Foundation gives applicants a pre-test test, and to date there's not any applicant successful in passing the preliminary test. Does this mean that the ability to discern is questionable? It's not by those who earn an income doing exactly the same thing. It's just that people who are committed to their work aren't anxious about displaying their achievements to prove an argument however, the Challenge is only available to judge whether you've honed your skills in the manner expected by Challenge organizers.

The issue isn't one of whether you are able to prove that you are psychic or even discern minds. The issue is whether or not you are able convince people who doubt your ability in a controlled setting. If you truly want to utilize your abilities to aid people, then establishing and honing your skills will assist you. For me scientists have more than established that people are able to read minds, and anyone can do it, even though there are some who haven't yet explored the possibilities. I'm aware that my ability to develop as a psychic just beginning but I also know the number of people it has helped , and that my motivations for studying the art are in all the right places. I'm sure that you're doing the same as well, because it's extremely enriching for your life when you can integrate compassion into your life and utilize it to aid people who are in search of the wisdom of your experience.

It is inevitable that there will be skeptical people. When it was announced in the history of the world that it was round it was laughed off by those who laughed at the notion. When space travel was being talked about in the old science film, these were just ideas people thought of but didn't realize that in the future, these ideas would come to realisation. But mind ability to read minds and psychic powers are utilized by people since the time that humans have been around. You might have noticed their names and attributed the term "prophet" and "seer" with the ability and those who saw visions of what was to come , and who could discern the thoughts of others like we are today. When this skill is acquired and it took certain prophets and seers for a long time to perfect their abilities and use it to benefit the world and that's the purpose all spiritual activities are meant to be used to serve. In many popular meditation techniques the concept is that the mind strives towards an enlightenment process and also utilizes an aspect of the brain that most won't ever discover since they don't seek it.

Enhancing your career

It is possible that your mind-reading and psychic abilities could be the answer to your goals in the future. If you think you could be psychic, or require to earn some sort of certification or to set yourself up as an expert There are organizations which deal with this type of accreditation. For instance, the Certified Psychic Society is somewhere where you can leave your mark along alongside other psychics. The organization allows psychics to promote their services. The most important aspect is that they offer different work fields in order to make sure that people searching for psychics will have one site to locate them.

The subject areas include:

* Entertainment

* Animal communicators

"Past Life Readers

* Professional Psychics

* Mediums

* Readers of Tarot cards

Of course , there are other fields and you could be one of them by advancing your abilities and proving that you are psychic and mind reader. Today, there are opportunities for all sorts of professions, and you could be able to see that once you start your journey towards psychic growth and mind reading that you truly have the ability to be capable of helping those in need of to help. Keep in mind that your goals must always be to honor your gifts you've been blessed with, and to be a part of the many others who have also joined the world of psychics, mind readers and others who have discovered how to use their senses to assist others.

Chapter 14: Developing Clairvoyance Exercises

This activity requires a lot amount of visualization, which it could be challenging if you aren't used to visually expressing and controlling the images you create.

Begin by picturing you are holding 7 balloons that match the rainbow colors. make them as vivid as you can. Orange, red, yellow and blue. Green, blue, violet, and indigo. Then you'll let each balloon go one at a given time. starting with the red balloon and wait until it is no longer see it prior to you release the next balloon.

The ability to imagine is beneficial for people who want to increase their clairvoyance as this is the way clairvoyants view images with their mind's eyes as still images or as little films playing in their heads. The more vividly you are able to think and imagine, the more easy you will be able to recognize the images the spirit world is sending to you when you apply your clairvoyant abilities.

After all the balloons are removed, Imagine a third eye in the middle on your forehead. It begins by being shut. Then it slowly opens completely. Keep this in mind regularly. It will prepare your mind to let you know how to make use of your clairvoyance to see what cannot be physically observed and can only be seen with your 3rd eye.

If you're worried that you're making up the meaning, then there's no need to be concerned. If the image is presented to you in a way that is not the need for force or having any control over it and making it behave as you wish it is indeed clairvoyant.

Make yourself feel safe from harm and that it's acceptable to have visions.

It is possible to go to an antique shop and purchase quartz crystal. Don't buy the first one you come across. Make sure to take the time to hold each. There will be one that speaks at you because it is yours. To improve your clairvoyance, you can lie down and place the crystal in the spot where your third eye is and then repeat the exercise. Quartz crystals will increase your abilities and assist in concentrating your abilities.

Engaging in creative visualizations when you hold certain crystals could assist you in the process of developing psychic or clairvoyant skills. Other crystals worth trying include amethyst in purple, which is a great beginner stone. Also, you can try white magnesite that aids in developing psychic visions and lavender fluorite, which helps you connect spiritually with your spirit guide and also helps you to see your visions clearly.

While you are meditating, you could be able to meet your guardian angel, your spirit guide, or both. It is because during meditation you're talking to your higher self as well as your higher self communicates with the realm of spirit. They are here to assist you, so try that you are grateful and thankful for all the assistance they provide.

Another imaginative way to visualize the scene is to visualize rain clouds and sun shining. Begin to imagine the rainbow in each color one at a moment, starting with red. When the color is clear and bright, the next color is likely to show up. When the rainbow is completed look at it in different ways, such as over a mountain, or as one whole circle or across the ocean, beneath the ocean, out in space, etc.

There are times when people beginning their journey, they keep their guard up throughout the day, and let their thoughts come to them at night , when they're in a state of dreaming. If you are having answers to the questions that you've posed when you awake the next day instead of in the daytime or during meditation, you have to note it. You should be able to discern the meaning in your dreams, as there are times when you must interpret them rather than believing that they are real instances, it is important to be looking for metaphors and then look at the dream from different perspectives to determine what it is really saying and how it relates to the situation in front of you. It is essential to be aware of the images that repeat themselves repeatedly.

A dream journal is essential. After waking, you should write down all the things you remember.

Try using an audio recorder if think it is more suitable for you. Then, you can transcribe it later.

You can find answers from your dreams by asking guides in spirit to guide you through your dreams. Before you sleep, make a request to your spiritual guide to grant you a dream that will help you solve a problem that you're dealing with, and let the guide understand that your open to any help they can provide to you. Next day, write down your thoughts in your journal and then express your gratitude in your spiritual guide's presence for their assistance in your desires. Sometimes, it can take many nights for the complete answer to be revealed, but just accept the fact that it might take a while and then thank them for their assistance.

Try making an enlightening prophetic dream time tea before going to bed. The primary ingredient is Mugwort that helps you to experience vivid and clear dreams. You can also include chamomile and lemon balm and lavender.

You can also make your own dream pillow. Dream pillows are tiny pillows with herbs in them to help soothe the sleeper and aid them to dream meaningfully. They are typically composed of linen, cotton or muslin. They are then filled with Mugwort and lavender, rose blooms, rose hops, chamomile as well as lemon balm and Mullein. The dream pillow shouldn't be overfilled. It is put into an envelope that is placed inside the case person who dreams and is expected to last for a couple of months.

Another option is to put certain crystals in your pillow crystals that can increase clairvoyance, let yourself talk to the spirit realm and also to help you have visionary dreams. Danburite can help you let go of anxiety and relax while helping you connect with the higher self and connect with your spirit guides . It also helps you understand the meaning behind dreams and meditation visions. Blue Kyanite helps make your abilities to see clearly and improve your connection with the spirit realm improves through the creation of lucid dreams.

Utilizing tools to assist you in improving your natural talents, as well as doing regular meditation and getting more attuned to your intuition and recognizing the messages that your guides from within give you and your clairvoyance will improve more accurate and you'll get more precise.

Auras and how to interpret They and How to Interpret

An aura is an emitted light that surrounds the body of an individual which is not visible to the naked eye but is visible as a kind of colored halo around the body of a person by mystic or psychic.

The aura may reveal a person's mood or their health condition by the color that it has. The aura of a person is usually multiple colors. It is possible to test this by having someone stand in front of a white background during light, and then look at the other side of the person. Let your eyes blur. There are times when you might observe more than one aura around the person. Sometimes, the aura may extend over their body, however, at instances, it is extremely within their bodies. In these instances they are protecting themselves and shutting their eyes. No matter what it is, an aura is something that can't be created. It is impossible to imagine yourself as an aura color. You are either a color or you aren't. The colors are easily changed based on the mood of the individual and the location they're. A happy, cheerful person with a vibrant yellow aura could arrive at their work place and then immediately switch to dull grey, just because they don't like the job they do but need to perform it in order to pay the bills.

There are four ways to examine an aura to make a decision about the energy it gives off. It is important to take a look at the colors, the consistency as well as the clarity and form and shape of your aura. There are specific meanings to every color of the aura that we will discuss in an entirely separate chapter. Primary colors are associated with their own definitions, while a mix of colors like the reddish brown color would depend into account the qualities of two hues. The clarity and brightness the color appears, can be crucial in the meaning, as the meaning of a bright color is quite different from dull colors.

When you are educated about hues, you'll also be able to be able to identify where on the body the color occurs. Each chakra is associated with a particular color so don't be amazed to see a color close to the chakra. Colors in one region can represent one thing while those surrounding a different part of the body could mean something entirely different.

When we examine an individual's appearance, we see their real self, all remains after you have removed all the mannerisms, habits as well as the person they pretend to be, as well as their petty, insignificant behaviour. The aura of a person reveals the person they really are, not just the person they appear to be anyone in public. In general the more well-balanced the aura the more healthy and stabilized the person .

While taking in the surroundings, you might find holes in certain places. This could be a sign of illness or injury and in other cases, the individual isn't aware of.

It is also possible to experience spikes that can result from an unintentional emotion or thought. Be aware when you interpret the aura that the spike is a sudden event that takes place and passes.

Read books about reading and understanding auras, then think of your own method to read the auras. Select and select what works and then use your senses to help you when it's time to perform an aural read for someone.

If you want to try out a new technique such that of reading auras practicing is the only way to master the ability. If you're practicing, and you believe you can see the color of a person, don't dismiss it up as an imagination. Make a note of what you saw , the time and location of your body. It is normal to see an inner aura of white when you are a beginner and as you keep working, you'll begin to notice other shades. This isn't something you can achieve and within a couple of days, you'll get it down. It requires some time and weeks of training So don't be discouraged when it's not happening immediately.

Practice by using an electric light with white shades, and the mirror to see yourself. Like all things, it's going to take some time. Start by looking at your neck, and then let your eyes get glazed over. As time passes, you'll be able to see the white aura within. When you let your eyes turn towards the outside and see if you can discern another hue? In time, you'll be able see the whole aura. If you have an extended mirror, you could be able observe shapes, various colors in various places.

In order to prepare for readings, it is beneficial to practice a meditation to prepare you to be able to sense the aura of the person you work with and also protect you from infiltrating the entire aura. When a client arrives with a negative mood or is worried about something. Practicing your meditation will prevent you from focusing on their emotions. It is possible to be compassionate however you don't have to be depressed.

The location you decide for your reading spot must be comfortable and a place where you feel secure and safe. Also, it should have plenty of light and not interfere with the work you are working on. A lot of people make use of the incense burner, smoke sticks crystals, and smudge sticks placed all over the space. It is a good idea to record the event on tape so that your client isn't distracted by notes when you're trying to finish the reading.

Spend just a few minutes with your client in a friendly conversations. Define the aura in case they aren't understanding then, when they're willing then light a white candle to symbolize the bond between you two and request that your guides from your spirit help you in this reading.

After the reading is completed, Ask the client if there are any issues that the client has not yet answered. Thank the guides of the spirit world for their assistance. Discuss what the client isn't understanding or any issues that have come up.

In this way, you can treat any injuries on the body or aura.

Cleansing Your Aura Before Conducting a Reading

Your aura could be a part of your clients to create the screen between you and your client. This will help to disengage your aura and prepare you to read the aura of your client. The meditation can also keep you safe from illness and emotions so that they don't get absorbed by you.

Before you meet with the client to you, be in a calm space for 15 minutes. Keep your back straight. If you'd like to play music, you are able to but it's best if it does not contain any words. Close your eyes, and then breathe deeply into your nostrils and to exhale out of your mouth. While you breathe in, you can imagine the bright white light coming from everywhere into your body. It will make it stronger and filled with energy. When you breathe out, you can you can say to yourself "I give up all my negative emotions stress, anxiety, and stress to the universe, where it will go away and never harm the living creature." As you exhale the smoke-colored breath that comes from your mouth. When you take your last breath, visualize an egg that is white light that is small at first but as it grows larger, it will be absorbed into your body. It will increase in size until it surrounds your body with its healing light. Nothing negative or evil will be able to penetrate it. Now imagine that a pair hands let you in to the egg which surrounds you. the hands belong to Your spirit guide. You can ask him to keep the door open so that you can read for your client, but remain safe.

Aural Colors

Red- A powerful character, greedy controlled emotional, self-satisfied materialistic, excellent leadership skills creative, sexually strong. Red pain can be treated but it'll hurt even longer before it can be better.

Crimson-passion and adultery, influencing sexuality, quarrelsome, and influential.

Scarlet-tempered, disdain angry and moody. It is also critical, sombre as well as superficial and difficult.

Maroonis strong determination and tenacious. He is temperamental, strong determined, strong, and victorious.

Pink- express your love with a gentle and kind manner, with kindness romanticism, love delicacy, respect ethics, perception, pleasure and having an open heart and also compromise.

Orange- A person who trusts their gut feelings, they are able to pick the feelings of others easily They're smart and are able to communicate clearly. They're attractive and flexible full of confidence and determination to accomplish their goals. They are also joyful and happy. They inspire, however, they also have the capacity to influence people, and they must be mindful to use this to their advantage.

Coralfertility, robust and robust.

Yellow- bright, healthy, cheerful, wealthy. This is a person who is skilled and innovative appealing, charming and convincing. They are generous and unattached to anything.

If the yellow appears dull, they're tired and in need of a boost. It may be related to the feeling of jealousy or betrayal. Anxiety, pain or outrage.

Greenis the color of love and fertility, as well as imaginative well-being, and health. The luck of the Irish is abundant and also finding love again and strengthening existing relationships. They have the natural ability to care for and help other people. Additionally, they have a deep love for the earth and are able to create anything to grow thanks to an enlightened green thumb.

If the green appears to be murky then there's a problem or problems with excess and even debauchery.

Olive- uncertain, conflicting and deceitful; lacking in strength determination, motivation and focus.

Ivy - emotional, faith anxiety, anguish, restorative and the ability to deal with the pain.

The color is greenish-yellow, which indicates fearfulness anger, gutlessness, anger and jealousy.

Forest Green - growth, the ability to earn a living, fertility, abundance in kinship, courage, and bravery with nature

Blue-Psychic abilities, intelligence peace, truth faith and justice. Blue-eyed survivors are born to fight the good fight They are fair, easy-going, and have the stamina to tackle everything that is thrown at them.

Dark Blue, spiritual bad habits hinder the person. Patterns that are established are difficult to get rid of. Neglect and carelessness.

Midnight Blue- wishes, dreams, hopes, wishes dreams, longings, ambitions and learning about magical arts.

Turquoise- They are active and vital. They are highly driven, and adept at inspiring others and convincing them to join in their cause. they excel in multitasking, and can arrange things in a systematic manner. They can easily become bored as they're constantly looking for the next thing to do.

Light Blue- loyalty, harmony, encouragement physical fitness and tolerance.

Indigo-astral activity that is likely lunar spiritual strength and wellness Self-awareness, good intuition.

Violetis a spiritual, deep thinker mysterious, ritualistic, and ancient wisdom

Nature, Brown-Earth new ventures, hesitation doubt, deceit imprudent, corrupt, can aid in discerning the truth even when others are lying, neutral, and peace. Unnerving confused, greedy and negative.

Gold - courage, allure and abundance, endurance, joy, faith in oneself, and success.

Grey-awareness, Give-and-Take glamour, protection from psychological attack. It also neutralizes and stabilizing dark depressing thoughts, uncertain intentions

Forces that are invisible to us such as fear death, binding coercion and negativity.

White-childhood The divine force of creation Pureness, beginnings integrity, truth, loyalty morality, honesty loving, restorative unity, and the creation.

Aural Shape and Texture

Aural Shape

An angular shape usually indicates that it's from another plane or sphere.

Animal-shaped shapes are often the animal that is the individual's spirit animal, or an attitude that they are trying to avoid which is similar to the specific animal. Shamanic individuals can alter their the auras of their animal spirit intuitively.

A sputtering of electrons in the aura show an absence of determination and self discipline. They want people to know what they experience and can feel also, which is why they put it out there for all to see and feel.

Shaped like a box, it usually means that the person is afraid and could be experiencing some sort of difficulty.

Continuously changing often indicates that the person is afflicted with strong emotions that can be changed at a moment's notice.

Flame shape often indicates that they have a magical inclination, and it is possible that they are experiencing a change in their knowledge of magic.

They are often easily accessible and self-assured.

Radiant refers to them as joyful and pure. These are the ones on the right track.

Spikey usually means that they're seeking to defend themselves, and are angry or outraged over something.

The way they dance can mean that their emotions are in the air, and they're confused.

Aural Texture

Dry could indicate that the vital force is declining as well as that the individual is filled with knowledge and wisdom, and the aura is drained. It's usually because of the hurt being too severe.

Fine and radiant happy people shoot glowing rays of light shooting out from their bodies with varying degrees of softness and completely blindingly. The texture is smooth and horizontal.

Mealy and Buttery are for people with generosity, helpful traits. They are mothering or friendly people who will offer the shirt off of their backs, when it's necessary. They're full of compassion for all animals and are willing to assist any person in need.

It appears as if people are covered with trash and usually is due to self-hatred. It could also be a person addicted to power and money and is deficient confidence in themselves. These individuals appear like massive pieces of mud that you would not be tempted to touch with a 10- foot pole.

There are a variety of ways to look at the aura, and it's up to you to decide how to interpret the results. Utilize your senses The first thoughts that occur to your mind are generally accurate.

Fantastic Techniques to Rejuvenate Your Aura

The aura you have is the part of you. When it's healthy, it's as a protective shield from any thing that may harm or harm you. Your aura must be strong, bright, and lively, so here are some ways to cleanse negative energy that has been exposed to.

The white sage's smoke is utilized to clean an area and rid it of any negative energy. It eliminates negative ions that are in the air. Use the smudge stick to move it upwards and downwards across your entire body, front and back to the extent you can reach without touching yourself with burning. I do this three times since the number is sacred.

Sea salt is extremely detoxifying cleaning your body and releasing you from stress. It is possible to go for an ocean swim in case one is near and then take a bath in sea salt. Or if do not have a bath, scrub your body with sea salt , and then take a refreshing shower that eliminates negative energy, cleanses dead skin, helps eliminate toxic substances, boosts circulation, and eases tension out of your body.

The sound is regarded by a lot of people as a healing tool. Choose a CD that contains Tibetan singing bowls that are renowned for their ability to disperse negativity and cleanse your energy. It is beneficial listening to these prior to getting ready to sleep.

Labradorite is a remarkable crystal that deserves to be mentioned. It can repair rips on the back of the body. If you hold it for 20 minutes, it can have an effect that lasts up to 12 hours. It is regarded as an energy stone that is worn by those who treat the body to provide to protect themselves. It's great used as bracelets.

Vertiver essential oil , when applied to the belly button prior to going to bed can prevent you to avoid using other people's problems to solve your own. It helps to calm you down and restore your equilibrium whenever you are feeling out of balance. It is an sedative and assists in aligning your chakras.

Black Tourmaline is a well-known stone to help eliminate negative energy. It's very safe and makes you feel safe, and can assist those who have many negative thoughts.

Angelsword flower essence is a source of healing as well. Fringed Violet flower essence helps to heal damaged or agitated auric fields. Drink it orally prior to going to bed.

Labrodrite is an excellent stone to wear when locations or people, or even certain circumstances cause you to feel depleted energy or tired. Make an effort to be as strict as you can, however, if it is not possible then don't allow yourself to be exhausted just because you must be in the area or in the vicinity of the person. Use the stone to keep off being depleted of energy and to protect yourself.

Aura Healing

If you're healing your own aura or who is healing their aura, you will be eliminating all the negative stuff that isn't needed or serves the greater good. You are activating and reviving the etheric body as well as each one of your chakras. When you heal your aura there's an obstruction or a weakness that you are working to improve. The blockage indicates that there is a large amount of energy held within a particular chakra or organ that can cause these areas to become affected and could cause illness physically. A lack of energy means that you don't have enough energy and must be replenished as well, which could cause illness.

In the areas that have a blockage, the blockage is eliminated by taking it out of the area that is damaged. This is followed by expanding therapeutic energy towards the region that you have just examined.

The most important aspect of blockages is to cleanse or disinfect. If there is deficiencies, it is necessary to restore and rejuvenating the chakras or affected areas, the focus should be placed on stimulating and energizing.

To determine the chakra of someone, let them lie down. Utilizing one of your hands and your fingers in a straight line and your hand should be straight, you'll slowly move your palm over a chakra while you breathe deeply, slowly exhale and in. Your hand will slowly move towards the person. The aura is about 4 inches higher than the body. It can appear as numbness when you've found it. You should be able to feel the seven major chakras.

If you are beginning an aura healing process, it's essential to request your spiritual guide to be with you to assist you with the healing. Archangel Michael is a suitable choice as he can protect the person you're healing and also you. The Arch Angel Raphael is the healing Angel therefore asking for his assistance is essential. Always request that your guide angels be in your midst to assist you. The energy you receive is a reflection of your goal. Therefore, anyone you request to be there can be found. Request that the person who is healing your higher self is there too.

If you are beginning an healing, it is essential to wash your hands. After that, sit down and shut your eyes, while repeating to yourself two times an invocation. It should be said with humility, love as well as gratitude, determination, concentration and modesty.

Please help me become an instrument for healing. Let compassion permeate my body for those suffering. Let your power of healing and renewal flow through my body I can assist those who are in need. I am grateful to you and acknowledge you with full confidence that you are there for me and will aid me in my efforts to get this person back to health.

Repeat the invocation twice Make it a heartfelt prayer, with faith and heart. Pause and be aware of the strength of the words. The next step is to create an aura security shield for the person you are healing , and surrounding you.

The area around my body with (other people's names) is the protection circle. It surrounds us, protecting us from negative energies. We are secure and safe within the circle.

Now is the time to invite the spiritual group you've asked to assist you.

Arch Angel Michael I request that you join me at this moment and during this whole healing. Please shield me and _____ from any evil entities or energy, or any negative thoughts, feelings or elements. Only allow in those who possess the brightest white light and only the best intentions for us. Please place us both in this circle of security, filling its with the pure white energy of healing and love that is guarding us and protecting us. I appreciate you and am thankful for everything you do.

Take a moment to pause for a few minutes, allowing him to come closer before he enters the circle. Imagine seeing him in the same place with your third eye open. See his energy flow out of his body into the circle. You can be sure that he's there with you, protecting and loving you. It's time to call into Arch angel Raphael.

Arch Angel Raphael I request that you be with me right now, and assist me through the entire healing process. Please guide me as I heal _____. Let your guidance and compassion to flow through my body, so I can heal properly _____. I am in love with you and am extremely grateful for everything you do.

Stop for a couple of minutes, allowing him to come closer before he enters the circle. Try to imagine him with your eyes open. Let his energy flow from him and into the circle. Be aware that he is with you, protecting and loving you. Now is the time to bring to your guide in spirit.

I would like to request that my spirit guide stay with me right now and through the entire healing process for _____. I ask you to guide me through this healing process for our highest and highest best. I am in love with you and am thankful for all that you do.

Take a moment to pause for a few minutes and feel him move closer before he enters the circle. Imagine that he is in the same place with your third eye open. Let his energy flow from his body into the circle. Feel that he's there, with you, protecting and loving you. In the next step, bring into the higher consciousness of your loved one that is being healing.

Higher Self of _____ request that you join me with me right now and go through the entire healing process. You can grant the healing energy to be absorbed in _____.

Allow the healing energy to assist _____ to achieve their highest goodness with grace. I cherish you and am grateful for everything you do.

While sitting, I lift my hands to my head, with my palms facing upwards. I then pray:

I now channel the incredible healing energy. The divine and exquisite healing energy flows through my body through my hands and arms and through my mind throughout my body's emotional system, into my etheric body, through my chakras, my aura and throughout my energy structure.

The energy is now building and increase when I take deep breaths. I breathe deeply and the chakras of my palms open to allow the energy to flow out of my heart through my arms, down my chest, out of my hands and then through to the heart of _____.

Inhaling 12 long, slow breaths, each one for 5 seconds before slowly exhaling. In the meantime I'm opening my hand chakras by putting the left hand into my right hand for 6 breaths, and then in the final 6 breaths, I'm pressing the right hand into my left.

My hands are full of energy. I turn off the light as I light two candle, one for the person in need of healing and the other to the team of spiritualists in the process of healing. Meditation music is played softly in the background.

Then, start by focusing on your crown chakra. It should be over their head approximately 3-4 inches. Place your left hand in a cup and move it from the crown chakra until the bottom. At the bottom of the feet of the person should be a bowl that is filled with water and sea salt. When you get to the feet, your cupped hand should dump negative energy into the salt water. It will repeat 13 times, going a bit higher each time you go to the bottom. The general sweep in the aura.

Then, you'll examine each chakra and organs of the body for energy that feels ill. This time , you'll be able to do a free scan, and if you notice something does not feel right, you can sweep the energy and then dump it into the water. Be sure to scan slowly so that you don't miss anything. After that, scoop it up and place it into the water. Repeat this process all the time you have to, until you no longer notice anything that needs to be get rid of.

After all positive energy is cleared off, it is time to cleanse the chakras with new healing energy. Return to the crown chakra of the head. Place your hands on the crown chakra, say:

The crown chakra of your body is restored, it's cleaned and clear of clutter.

Think of the chakra though you were staring directly at it. What do you see? You can imagine cleaning it gently, and seeing it shine and sparkle. You can see it completely clean and then say:

The crown chakra of yours is happy It's strong and can be repaired.

Feel yourself holding your hands directing energy towards the crown chakra. You can see white light flowing through your hands and into the chakra. Watch it vibrate and move while it is energized. Continue to send energy through your fingertips to your chakra.

The crown chakra of your body is moving freely and is fully in full open.

Take a look at the its twists. You will be amazed at the beauty as it expands. Next, look at the forehead, or Third eye chakra.

The Third Eye chakra is restored, it's cleaned, and is free of clutter.

Visualize the chakra if were staring directly at it. What is it like? You can imagine washing it, scrubbing it with gentle pressure, and then see it shine and sparkle. You can see it completely clean and then say:

The Third Eye Chakra in your body is joyful, it's solid, and can be repaired.

Feel yourself using your hands directing energy into the Third Eye Chakra. You can see white light flowing from your hands towards the chakra. Feel it vibrate and move while it is energized. Continue to send energy through your fingers to chakra.

The Third Eye chakra is open and is fully in a state of open.

Take a look at the it's twists. Notice how gorgeous it looks when it opens. Then, you can go to the throat chakra. Your Throat chakra, after all, is your Heart chakra, next your navel chakra, and finally, the basic chakra, and finally the your sex chakra. It is important to use similar words, and visualize the same thoughts for each chakra you're working with.

Feel the chakras clean and healthy. Imagine yourself washing them clean. Relax There is no need to hurry through this. Watch the chakras become filled with white light that is flowing out of your fingers and onto the person you are with. Watch the chakras' petal opening in one by one, and the light that comes from each chakra explodes when you turn and spin. Look around at the person who is being healed happy and full of happiness. They are no longer suffering from injuries or pains, and they're not anxious or sad no more. Say:

Your chakras are clean, restored and renewed. They are healthy, happy and restored. They are energized , stimulated and filled with white light. They are open and can move easily.

After saying these words, feel the chakras cleared. All chakras are happy and healthy. They are also repaired. They are stimulated and energized. They're all turning, glowing , and they have the most brilliant white that you've seen.

After a few minutes , say:

Arch Angel Raphael Please Arch Angel Raphael, I'm asking you to be with me today.

Begin to see him approach you. See his power and feel the emerald-green luminosity that is surrounding him. Smile and then wait for him to recognize you. Then say:

Arch Angel Raphael Please seal by emerald-green cleanse all the chakras, so that there are no leaks. The energies of _____ remain with _____.

Be on the lookout for him sealing each chakra at a time. You will see an emerald-green shield that surrounds each chakra, protecting it so that there are no leaks.

Thanks Arch angel Raphael to seal the chakras to ensure that the energy of _____ stays in them. Thank you for keeping an eye on the healing process and helping me to follow your guidance.

Thank you to the Higher Self of _____ for watching over my healing process and for helping me in my journey.

Thanks to the Spirit Guide for keeping watch over my healing and helping to guide me.

Thanks Arch Michael for your prayers. Michael to watch over my healing process and to me to protect myself and I am _____.

Sometimes but, there may be real gaps inside the aura. They could range from the size of a tiny dot to a massive gap. The holes can leave the person vulnerable to negative energies or thoughts that are negative, as well as negative effects. The cause could be intense feelings of anger or fear or alcohol, a drug habit physical trauma emotional attack, psychic problems, or even criticism from others.

If there's an energy gap in the aura, the person becomes depleted of energy. They may be able to be sick, suffer from migraines, or experience an abrupt shift in their mood. People are able to heal on their on their own, but at times they're not able to. Some people effortlessly steal energy from others They don't realize they are doing it, it's just what happens. If an energy hole is around someone in this way, the hole isn't going to heal. If the hole doesn't heal, it could be very dangerous. This leaves the person vulnerable to negative forces and physical and mental issues.

When you feel you have the appearance of a hole or tear If you feel a tear or hole, make circular motions over the region. Now you are playing more practical role. As you slide your fingers over the tear or the hole you should imagine the hole being closed and repaired. Watch and ensure there aren't any leaks, and that the hole is fully sealed, supported and rebuilt to ensure that, when you're done it's as if no damage whatsoever. In the future when you cleanse the chakra with pure white light opening isn't able to close again. Instead, the hole is sealed closed, but the chakra is opened by the white light, and it is complete and healthy, and is repaired. When you fix the tear or hole you examine the different layers over it for holes in the same spot as there are usually several that require repair as well.

Cleansing Your Aura after an Day of Reading

An ideal spot to clean your aura after a long day of reading is a relaxing bath lit by candles. The combination of fire and water stimulates growth and also helps to get rid of negative energy, unneeded energies and old, unnecessary issues. A tiny amount of moon charged salt can work equally well. Imagine the water glowing in white and as you slide into it all your negative black energy, the stress of the day disappear, gradually becoming lighter until they're white too.

Make a bag with sage and thyme as the water runs to cleanse your aura.

The salt must be charged with moon energy, then held towards the east, and then asked to be cleansed. It will benefit both the aura and the mind and astral body.

Hospitals advise salt baths as they cleanse and naturally fight off bacterial infections. There is also a belief that salt removes physical trauma-related memories and astral bodies. Salt is a nutrient that helps your body, since it's an element that is earth-based It cleanses and acts as a type of protection.

Before you go in the bath, visualize yourself making an imaginary circle around the bathtub. The objects in the circle are sacred and protected. The importance of visualization is paramount when it comes to this. It is important to imagine yourself entering the circle and into the bath, releasing everything negative, letting them go and calming them so that they won't hurt any other person. If you have any negative feelings that might have been transmitted to you by people whom you read for, they will melt away and transform into pure white light coming into your body. If you feel like you're energized and you no longer feel negative thoughts in your mind It is the time to get out of the spa and the circle by thanking it for its protection and clearing you of any negativity. Also, thank your guide in spirit for their assistance. After that, you must remove the circle. Then, as the water flows through the drain, imagine the negativity removed forever.

Clairvoyance as well as Reading as well as Healing Auras are something anyone can master. It's a process that takes time, patience and many hours of practicing. However, if you are determined to go after them they are achievable. Anyone has the potential but they must do the work.

Chapter 15: Guerilla Meditation

Do you have a difficult getting over your emotional turmoil? Do you require a way to help ease anxiety?

Are you struggling to keep your focus? Make a difficult decision? Are you feeling the pressure of the day accumulating? Do you require a unique solution? If so you're in need of a quick meditation session, then a few minutes could be exactly what you're looking for.

Meditation has been receiving much attention in recent times because of its claims to the enhancement of clarity, focus, as well as stress-related physiological and emotional reduction. The ability to stay conscious and present that results from meditation is becoming a technique for leadership in and of itself. Meditation comes in many forms but the purpose is identical: silence the mind. But I've noticed that powerful active people require several ways to achieve this level of concentration.

In this article, I'd like present to you one of my most-loved techniques for guerilla meditation: the five-minute Guerilla Meditation. This is an example, followed by a step-by-step instruction on applying this method for yourself.

Be aware of your breathing throughout your day. It could be during the time you're talking or meeting with friends or when you notice yourself becoming stressed or overloaded with too much work with not enough time or when you become stressed and distracted. Set a timer and test these suggestions:

Begin by sitting down and lay your feet down on the floor. Take a look at the soles of your feet and observe how they are connected to your thighs, shins and torso, sit bones and backbone, neck, shoulders as well as your head and arms. It's a brief body scan to focus your focus on your body.

In the end, pay attention to the way you breathe. Do you breathe shallow or deeply? Where in your lungs do you use (upper the chest area, in mid-belly lower belly, or back)? Are you breathing fast and to achieve this, perhaps lifting your shoulders or putting them on your stomach? What is the pattern in your breath?

Begin to breathe by slowly taking a breath to your belly, then reduce it to your back. Don't push yourself too hard. If breathing through your stomach isn't your thing, begin your breath in the upper chest rather than the lower. It is imperative to repeat your self, "breathe in and breathe out" while your mind might wander. Return to the exhalation and inhalation, with no judgement in case your focus diverges.

When your timer starts to tick you should take a few minutes and write your goal for the future in your head.

It doesn't need to take much time or require special training to reap the benefits of mindfulness. It is possible to begin today and right now and even now. Take your deep breaths and look at what happens.

The importance of staying the Same

Anyone with an empathic personality should be happy because they'll always have someone to help them understand their feelings before they express their feelings. Empaths have a distinct skill: the ability to convey emotions and feelings in a more efficient way than other people. This is among the reasons they are excellent friends. However, not all people are right to be a part of their circle. This is because there are some people who simply think of their own self and nothing other than themselves. They try to convince people to change their emotional beliefs. If you truly love someone's company, they'll never ask you to change and you should not change just because you want to be a great partner.

Change only if you feel it's the best for you to change your mind. You will always have people in your life who are not happy with the present you're giving. These people will hate you until you are the person they wanted to be. You may begin to question your mental health or your sensitivity. There is a possibility that you'll feel pressured as an empath to change yourself to make others feel at ease around them, but this is not required. This is among the most valuable learnings you'll acquire and you must never forget your personal values to please another person.

It could be thought of in a different light. It's manipulative to make a decision to alter yourself simply because someone else is liking you. You're causing the person to examine your behavior and decide if they'd like to keep dating you. Your partner may never see the true you and that's a shame.

Be Prepared to Protect Your Empathic Needs

Being an empath, you'll probably face many obstacles throughout your life. The feeling of being emotionally exhausted is your constant companion. If you're seeking to deal with it, you first need to be aware of your needs to empathize and fulfill these needs. You have to determine ways to guard against the fears that you are experiencing. You may encounter people who ask excessively of you. If you've got individuals in your life that make you feel emotionally compelled to do something you do not want to, you can tell them "No." If you're unable to stay for longer than two or three hours without having a social gathering do not push yourself to the limit. Be sure to have your vehicle prepared to ensure that you don't get stuck where you've been. Always have a backup plan of transport so that you can get to your destination whenever you're feeling like it.

You may ask your companion not to wear it if are sensitive to strong smells or certain scents, and should someone wear it, be sure to sit away so that you're not impacted by the smell..

Also, consider taking short breaks in between to get fresh air.

If you are overwhelmed by large groups there are some ways to help you stay in the right direction. One of the most effective strategies to do this is eating food that is high in protein prior to attending an event where there are likely to be many people.

Always find a quiet room in your house where you can relax and not be distracted.

Finding the things that hurt You and Find Time to Reconnect with You

The unique energy empaths experience in their daily lives can be exhausting or rejuvenating. They can encourage personal development and keep your emotional well-being when it's rejuvenating. If you are experiencing a draining experience and the empath is unable to cope, it will get exhausted. The most effective method to determine the cause of fatigue is to maintain a journal. It is possible to write down your thoughts and feelings in your journal without fear of being judged as it permits you to note the things that you perform on a daily basis. This will help you in identifying what's driving your emotional drain.

Many people believe that the only thing that boost empaths are yoga and meditation as per one of the popular myths. However, this notion is not true. Every aspect of your life could inspire you. If you like taking pictures for fun, doing it could be beneficial for you. If, however, you love cooking, bake cakes or cookies to see if your energy levels rise.

Whatever can make you feel happy However, there are occasions in your day which completely drain you. It could be that is as easy as to the grocery store during busy times or using public transport when it's full. It could be anything from a conversation with your spouse when you return from work to making plans to deal with the issues. It is easier to create the appropriate arrangements to react in the event you are aware of what is draining you. It is then possible to create tasks to manage these events and boost your level of energy.

Do you get enough time to yourself? If you don't then you must take action now to change things? Empathy is among the most amazing qualities that exist in the world, however, if it is not controlled it could slowly degrade the empath from inside out. It is important not to allow other people to profit from your positive manner of thinking. It is a sour experience when an empath's positive emotions are reacted to with a sense of manipulation and vengeance. The empath's spirits will be burdened due to all of this. The reason why empaths must to prioritize themselves.

The meaning of ASTRIAL TRAVEL, ITS TRASPORTATIONS AND ITS

Astral travel is now associated with astrology, as well as other forms of research that are based on the motions of celestial objects such as planets and stars.

Astrology is the idea that celestial bodies, like the stars or planets, exert an influence over human affairs.

Astrologers believe that certain events in the lives of people can be influenced by circumstances beyond their control. A majority, if not all of them are spiritualists , or even occultists. They believe in telepathy, extrasensory perception as well as other similar concepts which were once associated with spiritualism.

Astrology has always been a major element of pseudoscience. In recent years it has gained popularity with the general population.

Astrology websites have increased in popularization, and the astrologers as well as believers are becoming more prominent on television as well as in newspapers.

With the number of books on astrology that are published each year, it's easy for anyone with no background knowledge to understand the subject.

Spiritual journeys are those where a person develops spiritually. The word "spiritual" is a reference to consciousness or human awareness and not physical senses in this instance.

No matter what religion or belief the possibility of spiritual growth is there. It usually involves self-reflection and self-discovery. One who has developed spiritually could have a greater degree of mental health as well as a better knowledge of the universe or a connection to more than the ordinary world.

Spiritual journeys, similar to physical trips, can be scary at times. They could involve leaving familiar terrain and moving into an unfamiliar, perhaps dangerous environment.

A lot of people who start on a spiritual journey face fear and doubt on the path. These feelings can cause the journey as if it is difficult.

A person who views the world as an exciting adventure could follow their spiritual path the same manner as they would face any other challenge in their life.

At first glance at first, astral travel and spiritual experience may seem to have nothing in any way. They do have some similarities. A trip, spiritual or physical is involved. Both trips could be a bit scary at moments.

Both trips require courage and determination. Both require faith and confidence to endure the journey.

Astral travel differs from spiritual development by one crucial aspect: we need to go out into the world to meet with others in order to gain delight and learn.

Many people who are not comfortable with social interactions struggle with astral travel. Certain people who are not able to find a job that is suitable might be reluctant to search for one and start an alternative career.

In this case the astral journey is seen as too terrifying and challenging to attempt and prevents the person from making progress.

Spiritual growth However, the process of spiritual growth requires no human interaction. Many people enjoy spending time reading on their own about their faith, or visiting holy places.

This is among the reasons spiritual growth could be more difficult than traveling through astral space.

THE SEVEN CHAKRAS AND THEIR IMPLICATION

The Seven Chakras are energy bodies situated in the body's most inner areas that transport and distribute the life force. The chakras are connected to different glands, organs, hormones, reproductive processes and minerals. If they're off-balance or imbalanced chakras can influence physical as well as spiritual health.

If you are experiencing emotional blockages such as depression or anxiety, then making use of Reiki healing to tune your chakras can be beneficial.

It is believed that the Seven Chakras can be placed in your body's energy fields. The chakra system can also be used to direct and control the way one experiences life. It can be utilized similarly to the hands and fingers to make a variety physical gestures. They assist in detecting and integrating external movements into our conscious.

It is crucial to understand how chakras are linked to one another in order to comprehend how they impact each other. There are three levels:

1. Physical

2. Etheric

3. The spiritual

The seven chakras are:

Root Chakra (Muladhara)

It's located near the base of the spine within the pelvic region. It is responsible for our instinctual being the home and family environment and a sense of belonging and how we deal with challenges within our daily lives. The final chakra, called known as the Throat Chakra, represents your connection to Earth. When our spiritual work is completed, we need to come back to our Throat Chakra.

Sacral Chakra (Svadhisthana)

This is the force that controls the way we feel sexually, enjoy ingenuity, creativity and the way we handle the challenges of life. It is situated in the lower part of the spine. This chakra, known as the crown chakra, is final to be activated within our energetic system. It is the way we perceive our own self. When the chakra is fully open it will be clear what we are and why we're on Earth.

Solar Plexus (Manipura)

It's located at the belly button. It controls the way we interact with others, in addition to aggression and anger, leadership capabilities and proactive behaviour in daily life. This chakra is connected to elements of fire and it's the place to return once our spiritual journey has ended.

Heart (Anahata)

It's located on our chests. It controls the way we treat others, love with others, and how we express our self to other people. This chakra is linked to that element called air because it helps us feel spiritually liberated and offers us a the feeling of being free throughout our lives.

Throat (Vishuddha)

In the throat the throat chakra controls the capacity of our throat to communicate with other people. This chakra is associated with elements of Ether and is the place where we connect with Spirit.

This chakra located within the Etheric as well as Spiritual degrees, has been situated on the spinal column towards the other side. The etheric level is the blue lotus flower that flickers. Once the spiritual level has been attained, the blue lotus will only appear.

Third Eye (Ajna)

The chakra that is situated between our eyes. It controls the way we perceive and comprehend the world around us, as well in our ability to understand and handle visualisation. The light element is linked to the chakra. It helps us think rationally and with a higher level of intelligence.

Crown (Sahasrara)

The pineal gland, which is located on the top of the skull regulates spiritual growth spiritual awareness, cosmic awareness, as well as awakening. This chakra is linked to the element of ether, which permits us to be more spiritually developed state.

The chakras of the seven can function as emotional and psychic energy centers, too. The root chakra is linked with feelings of security as well as security and happiness When the chakra is blocked or imbalanced you may feel vulnerable and uncomfortable. The voice, which is our capacity to express our emotions and express our feelings is linked to the chakra of our throat. If we aren't in balance we may struggle to meet our needs.

Third eye chakra is also known as the sixth chakra (the third eye) and is a source of psychic energy, and is connected with the pineal gland. It is possible to have dreams that appear more real in comparison to others when associated with this chakra, or you may experience awake visions during sleep.

The Power of CHAKRA Balance and Healing

Chakra-based healing is gaining a lot of interest however, the question is what is exactly it? In Sanskrit, chakra means "wheel" or "vortex." This is the center of energy which circulates life energy around and throughout the body. The chakras, found all over all of the body's parts from top to bottom, and work together as teeth in a gear and function as cogs. You feel rejuvenated and well-being when every chakra is functioning at maximum efficiency. If the chakra is not in balance it can cause emotional and physical symptoms that range from minor to serious. There are a variety of methods to ensure the balance of our chakras. Certain healing techniques increase the frequency of our chakras. others shift energy between them.

If we're stressed our chakras can concentrate on just one chakra at one time. If we're relaxed and relaxed, we are able to freely shift between chakras to get to the next. Seven chakras as explained, are all nested within another and possess various meanings and therapeutic purposes. The chakra of your head is for instance, which governs your mind and the belief system. On the other hand, your root chakra is responsible for Earth energy and grounding, as well as resistance to negative energy. The chakras are connected to colours and regulate specific feelings and abilities.

1. Its Root Chakra (red) can be linked with fear and worry.

2. Relationships and self-esteem are both dealt with through the Sacral Chakra (orange).

3. The Solar Plexus Chakra (yellow) -Willpower and personal energy.

4. Green Heart Chakra is associated with compassion, love creativeness, intuition, and creativity.

5. The Throat Chakra (indigo or blue) is a channel for manifestation and communication.

6. Third Eye Chakra (purple) is a symbol of wisdom and intuition, psychic ability.

7. "The Crown Chakra" (white) symbolizes the spiritual connection to God's energy.

The Chakras and the Healing power of Sacred Geometry

We'll use sacred geometry in order to make a healing space for each chakra, using the science of color and. Each shade has its very own unique vibration that is compatible to the chakras that we'll send our unique colors to treat them. The exercise can be completed either by yourself or in groups, so long as you're only working with one person.

To start to heal your chakras, you can utilize chanting and singing to relax and calm your mind in order you can connect to them. If you're performing this practice in a group, this process will take about five minutes. If you're working on it alone you should set aside 15 minutes. Crystals, candles, tuning forks, and various things can all be used for creating an energizing space for meditation. The more harmony and color you can bring to your surroundings the more effective.

If it is resonating within your body, your chakras are healing and you're now in a position to take your next step. Every chakra will be connected to vibration and color for the next color as it is able to resonate, with the intention of healing and balancing them.

OPENING UP YOUR THIRD EYE CHAKRA

It's like you're peering out of the curtain of ordinary reality into an unimaginable realm when the Third eye chakra is opened. This is referred to as the omniscience or awakening. Third eye chakras are a mysterious channel that connects us with our spiritual and higher self as well as the universal wisdom. It's the entrance to the realm of the spirit.

When you are able to activate your third eye chakra you will experience a major impact on your daily life. It is possible that you will open in unintentionally, but it's for your greater good. Many metamorphoses will happen when you unlock the third eye chakra from inner peace and wisdom to dazzling psychic abilities that are superior to those who are not as advanced in their spiritual understanding to extend beyond this world and into other realms or dimensions.

You'll be able to see or sense psychic energy angels, spirits or other entities, as well as human auras when you have your third eye chakra being open. It will be possible to perceive things from a different perspective, and your otherworldly vision will be transparent. You might even discover how to see even in darkness. Your spiritual vision is beyond distance and time. If you notice a clear shift in your consciousness, your third eye chakra opens..

What will happen if you Close Your Third Eye?

There will be a major change in your life. You'll be able to feel the energy of everyone when you learn the techniques to open your 3rd eye. You'll be able be able to see angels, ghosts, monsters, and demons that could harm or annoy you. It's possible to see what's going on on another side. You might also get some info directly directly from the beings or entities from an alternate dimension. If you encounter an entity, be at peace. Don't get caught up in fear about what's to come. It is possible to experience prophetic events or nightmares. You may also experience dreams of the spiritual realm.

A lot of people will be intrigued by this book because it shows an awakening spiritually that provides individuals with a fresh perception of their own and the lives of others. It is a sign of spiritual awakening and extraordinary psychic abilities.

When you keep the Third Eye open it will be possible to see energies that other people aren't able to, such as angels, spirits, and spirits from other realms or dimensions. Lucid dreams are also possible.

Meditation for the entire body Within the Aura

The meditation on the inner-aura body increases your spiritual energy and assists you use it to increase the abilities of your psychic. Begin by sitting comfortably in a sitting position. Close your eyes and imagine yourself being surrounded by an airy layer around your body. Imagine the shape and color of your ideal job. Think about the energy that extends 3 feet to all directions, beyond the physical body.

The violet aura shields you from the evil spirits, psychic energy, as well as bad entities. It also grants psychic power over other people because they aren't able to get access to your mind as quickly.

If you begin to be infused with spiritual energy via meditation, yoga or other activities that promote spirituality your aura will begin to become apparent.

OVERVIEW OF THE MAIN DIFFERENT TYPES OF SPIRIT GUIDES

Spirit guides or spirit guides are among the subjects that we've been discussing throughout this book. Another useful tool for the psychic is spirit guides, whether you want to meditate to ground yourself and recharge your energy, gather more strength before you begin reading, or seek assistance/protection--all of which are reasons to attempt to connect with your spirit guides and ask them for advice and strength. If you are requesting something you need, make sure to be courteous and respectful. Don't demand anything from them, instead do not be frightened or embarrassed to seek help since we cannot do everything on our own.

Your guides, or whatever you want to identify them, the word is very clear: they're not gods you need to worship. They are spiritual beings who is watching over your life and guides you. There's no need to worry about the gods of vengeance, they're there for you and will do only the best for you!

There are several different types of guides from spirit. Your guide could be an ancestor or loved one who has passed away from physical existence but still watches over you. If they're relatives it could be someone who passed away before your birth However, certain clues appear when family members mention that they're nearby. For instance, if there was the grandmother who loved flowers and flowers were a common feature in your life, this could suggest that an ancestor is looking after you.

Ancestral spirits can be able to trace their roots for several generations. If you are in contact to them, you may not be able to see their faces however you will feel an emotional connection and connection. It is possible that you are accompanied by a loved one who died who died in your life. It's likely to be someone who passed away before you, since spirits are believed to keep watch over you throughout all of your existence, however, it could be someone who passed away after you did.

Your spirit guide might not be a member of your family or come in the form of a symbol. It could be simply pure energy that appears as a glowing shining light. Archangels and angels are the two types of entities. It's possible that they're an energy that is soothing and a known entity that's been there to help you since the time the moment you came into this world. You must ensure that the entity that you're connecting to is indeed your guide to spirit. If there's any indication of dark or discomfort this isn't your guide spirit. The only time you interact with your guide/s is enjoyable. That's how you can tell for absolute certainty.

There are spirits of light who are referred to as spiritual guides, in addition to archangels, angels, and ancestral spirits. They aren't celestial because they were human at one time, but they serve the same functions as archangels and angels providing guidance, advising and guarding you. They're not always people you've met or loved.

Let's explore how you can connect and connect with your guides' spirits after you have learned the fundamentals. It could be your first experience with your guide. You may not know the appearance they will adopt!

The majority of people's preferred method of communication with their spirit guides is to do meditation. There are a variety of guided meditations to communicate through your spiritual guide. If you're not practicing an enlightened meditation, concentrate on connecting with your spirit guide as you meditate. It is also possible to focus on the goal you'd like to talk with them about in case you're contacting them to discuss a specific issue. Start by focusing to connect with your spiritual guide, and then concentrate on the subject that you would like for them to address. Relax your mind and avoid pushing things. Don't get upset in the event that something doesn't go as planned immediately, just like every aspect of spirituality. Keep seated to be in a state of meditation with the desire to connect with your spiritual guide. They may not show up within your vision or appear as an image but when you keep your mind open and clear the presence of them will slowly appear to you and your connection to them will increase in time.

Sometimes, your guides may appear to you even if you are not in a state of meditative or on a course or even reaching towards them, for instance, an owl flying in to directly on the road that you were walking along and focusing its gaze on you or your grandmother's scent immediately filling your nose for a short time or hearing a tune you've always thought was about your uncle, who died. You may be witnessing things in the path that don't exist. It could also be the bright light, the fresh air in your body and goose pimples. They could all be indications of your guides and their presence.

It might be your angel of protection providing tips or advice in your daily moments when your gut instincts strongly prompt you to act or to not do something (similar to the clairaudience). This message doesn't require you to take action and all you need to do is listen and take the advice. In the spirit world the guide you have is probably aware of the things you're not aware of, and may have information that you do not, therefore it's always wise to believe in them. However, in the end, it's ultimately your choice. They're not tyrants, rather they're guides.

If you've had dreams the spirit guide/s might make an appearance. If you've experienced a vivid or unique dream that a calm entity (whether it was your deceased grandmother or an animal, or an energy presence) spoke to you, communicated with you or guided you to something or someone and you recall it immediately the next day, or at least recall the main points that they've been saying and demonstrating to you, it was probably the visit of the spirit guide. Although you might remember the images you saw , and the things that were spoken to you after you woke up, you're likely to lose important details--if not the entire dream as the time passes It's an excellent idea to keep your dream journal and write down the details of your dream in the most detailed way feasible after you wake up. If you have to go out to work, it's possible to keep a notepad on your phone but it doesn't need to be anything spectacular. You can copy the notes into a notebook at any time to keep track of your spirit guides, creative or important dreams. If you'd like to connect with an angel guide in your dream, think about the question you'd like to be to be answered or the motive behind contact with them prior to getting ready to go to bed. As you fall asleep, sleep with this idea in mind, you might dream about them in the night. This is a way of dreaming lucidly, but be careful not to become too attached to it immediately.

It's possible to establish an unbreakable connection and channel for contact through your guide's spirit, no whatever form or shape they are in. By practicing, you could accomplish this. Keep in mind that if an individual or location that you consider to be your spirit guide causes you to feel bad or is infused with negative or dark spirit, it's not the spirit guides you have. Positive interactions with guides is always the best option, particularly if they're a deceased relative's ghost, or perhaps a sweet. Your spirit guide or guardian angel will only want only the best for you, and could be a great source of help to not ignore.

HOW DO YOU CONNECT TO YOUR SPIRIT GUIDES

Guides to the spirit realm are groups of souls that were created by God to protect against all evil. Meditation and prayer are among the most popular ways to connect with your guides spiritually. Engaging with natureor practicing yoga are also alternatives. Since the moment we first stepped foot on the earth and they've been guarding us. We're no longer the sole ones after being born. When you're born, you've been given to be taken care of and guided in a manner which you are unable to achieve independently. Your guardians are your primary caregivers. When you interact with one for the first time after birth, you receive a blow to your head. This is also a message of blessings and great joy along with huge difficulties and suffering, as the majority of things in life. The wise old owl can be very helpful to human beings. They'll always be at your side when you contact them in need of help. It's essential to know how to speak to them to help and defend you throughout your everyday life.

First step to acknowledge that they exist , and that they exist to serve your needs. Imagine them as long-lost family members who are always willing to listen to their suggestions whenever it comes into your life.

Relax your eyes as you contemplate and unwind. Visualize yourself sitting in a sacred location, bathed in all the colors that the night sky has to offer. Relax and let your thoughts guide you to a location near a waterfall, where angels can be found lounging or flying around. There's music on and everyone is having fun at the celebration and singing praises to God. You are able to choose every aspect of the sounds, sights as well as the smells and emotions that you feel while lying on a cushion or with the breeze moving through your hair as you fly through the sky with angels.

As you wander around in your dreamy world let yourself breathe deeply and enjoy an easy stroll. Watch the glow in people's eyes and feel their laughter. Feel the wind at your fingers as you run across the grassy banks that lie close to the edge of the waterfall, and take in the mountain fresh air as it falls from the top. It's like you're there and gradually rise up as you're ready to break free from your meditative state.

Prayers can be offered alone or with the company of. While you are going through your day all around the world, ask to your angels to protect and surround you. They will help you when you reach out to them when you need help.

Another method to connect with your guides in spirit is to practice yoga. In yoga, we stretch our bodies and focus our minds on calming while breathing deeply and slowly throughout our body. Yoga offers a wide range of benefits and uses that range from physical to spiritual. The most appealing thing is the fact that, as you do it, the more aware you will be of the feeling of peace and peace which comes from connecting to your inner angels.

There are many ways to communicate with your guides, however I suggest you select the type and mode of communication that is appropriate for you.

Connecting to your spiritual guides will establish the foundation for joy in your daily life. You'll feel secure throughout the day, and be able to get help and guidance if you require it. Every step on your journey it is clear that you're loved by the world.

CONNECTING TANCE SPEAKINGS

Certain theologians believe that following passing away, the soul goes into the state of limbo in order to determine if it has fulfilled its duties on earth and is now ready to return. The soul is believed to depart from the body once the body has gone and ghosts are believed as souls who are not yet gone.

The term "trance" is derived from the Latin word meaning "to drift." Trance states can be created by an hypnotic state, and is usually performed with music. Certain people are able to be put in a trance upon command, while other people may enter one by themselves.

When channeling passively the conscious mind of the channeler is transferred to the entity that he or she is trying to connect with. The channeler is an instrument of passive transmitting of messages or information like automatic writing, but is different from automatic writing in the sense that the information is not created directly through an unconsciously occurring process. The channeler could or might not be aware of their encounters with the spirits. They could or may not be able to describe their experiences.

When there is an active channel, the person who is channeling is believed to be engaged in a conversations with another person. The information channeled was created in a deliberate manner and contributes to the knowledge of a third-party. In this scenario, "channeling" can refer to one particular event of active channeling and the ongoing communication between a medium and spirit.

The concept of a spirit is that they be able to transmit diverse information, like health or world issues, in addition to the past lives of.

Also, it is possible spirit may assist people with overcoming difficult emotional challenges. In addition psychics have the belief that spirit guides could offer advice and guidance in this world as well as the afterlife.

Spiritualists make use of alternate states of mind to discover details about a particular person or loved ones they lost. Spirit communicaters may also attempt to communicate with people who are still in The Other Side, but this is not as common.

Many spirit mediums believe in the power of spirits to act as autonomous beings , and don't consider this process as a method of communication, some believe that it is possible. Spiritualist writers like Arthur Mather, Alvin Boyd Kuhn as well as Eusapia Palladino have written about the ways in which they felt "channeled" from spirits. The year 1910 was the first time British psychical research researchers conducted tests on Palladino in a séance. Palladino was believed to be devoid of influences by her experimenters according to the researchers and did not use any method they knew about.

Mediumship is a catchy term that refers to various different mediumistic methods. The word "mediumship" includes both "passive" as well as "active" kinds of mediumism.

The people who believe they see ghosts or hear voices but think they're not the person who is causing their perceptions and might or may not understand what's reported participate in passive forms mediumship. The person who allows communication to occur may believe they are hearing a voice message or message coming from spirit. Mediums are believed to be in contact with spirits or spirits when they practice active mediumship such as channeling.

ASCENDED MASTERS, THEIR MESSAGE AND THEIR MASTER

The term "ascend" can mean two things: (1) to rise from a common or low source to the top or more noble position and (2) the act of rising from such an beginning. Overcoming all negative forces and becoming spiritually enlightened is the best advancement on the planet. It's only because of massive effort that we will be able to achieve this, and for that we must dedicate our whole self to the Creator. This is the ultimate aim of spiritual growth and the most valuable service we can give to God.

The appearance of the Ascended Master in the world of Earth will be 10 times more powerful than in the history of mankind, as the universe is shifting to a higher frequency. This is because of an awakening in consciousness throughout the world. People who are becoming conscious of the spiritual side of life and questioning their motives for existence are driven to figure out exactly what is true.

Are you looking to find out the more you know about your life and your real motives? Learn this course in three parts that will take you step by step to an increased level of consciousness. Learn to harness the energy codes within your mind to lead a happier life.

Who reaches Nirvana

The Ascended Masters are beings of light who have successfully completed the sixfold paths of Light in the spiritual dimensions. They are currently on the way to heralding a new era on Earth. They've spent the past two centuries helping humanity through the transition to a higher frequency and in discovering the the truth within.

As like Jesus who was their Lord, they have given their lives to spread spiritual wisdom for the entire world. They aren't "dead," but rather have been able to ascend through death's gates into the realms of spirituality. They are able to assist humanity in its journey towards the future of awakening in all levels of this level.

What is an Ascended Master?

A Ascendent Masters is an spiritual leader who has achieved a high level of consciousness. They can be within the physical realm in a conscious and alert way. They have gained control over their own consciousness and are able to freely travel between dimensions. They remain fully within their bodies and act as a guide for others who want to follow their path. Sentient beings that have higher levels of consciousness are referred to as enlightened ones known as ascended masters or bodhisattvas.

People who are enlightened and have attained this level of consciousness may remain in the physical realm and therefore are referred to as

Ascended Masters. The Ascended Masters are blessed with a greater spectrum of capabilities that the ordinary person who lives on Earth. They are much more educated and can perform extraordinary things in and outside of the physical world. For instance, these masters could make people, places or objects experience amazing phenomena and then take residence in the dreams of people.

These Masters are directly connected to the spiritual aspects of each individual being in the universe and hold significant influence over the spiritual development of both nations and cities. The Ascended Masters assist individuals in accepting and recognizing their true nature, so that they can ascend to a higher state of being.

HOW TO HEAL YOURSELF and OTHERS

Healing Mediumship is the ability to heal yourself and others by utilizing the assistance of spirits. It addresses physical, mental emotional, spiritual, issues with karmic origins, and so on.

An energy treatment that can correct any imbalance between these parts of us is known as Healing Mediumship. You will experience a smooth ride from beginning to end. Healing mediumship can be used to find peace within your life and receive unconditional love by your Angels.

Healing is a crucial aspect of every day life. This is by far the most effective way we as humans can use to confront reality and reach our personal goals. You could get help from your spiritual guides to help you and others heal. This can happen in many ways:

You can use your intuition to channel the Universal Life Force Energy into people who need to heal to serve a variety of reasons and motives as a self-healing method that produces change using your personal energy.

You can also seek help by your guides who can assist you or anyone else. They will help you navigate the process while you are in an altered or spiritual mental state.

Healing is something that we all have the capacity to accomplish. It's in our genes to be capable of healing. It's part of being a human. If you're born with the ability to connect with health or not, it is a fact that you will definitely end up healing someone else at one point in your life. It's usually performed to help people or to respond to a situation.

You can serve as the link between someone who is in need of healing and your spiritual guide or angel who can perform the treatment.

The healing process can also occur in a group situation which is when they sit in a circle and form the foundation of a healing field.

Additionally, you can help in healing animals. Pets that heal themselves may have superior results than healing humans because they don't have the mental structures or mental obstacles that hinder the human body's ability to heal. I am always crying in my sessions of animal healing as I watch these sweet animals surrender to the healing energy. A few of them go into the state of trance, and others sleep or lay down their head on my shoulder or my foot.

Any kind of healing method that is healing-related, like Reiki, Healing Touch, Therapeutic Hands-on Healing etc. can be used.

According by Doctor. Doreen Petersen of the Mayo Clinic in Rochester Minnesota, is the most effective method of self-treatment: "Self-medication to heal your body and mind could be inexpensive and simple. "When suffering from persistent pain, you might find that it is possible to treat this on your own. It's a type of physical therapy can be used whenever you need." The reality that we all require healing regularly will not come as a shock when you consider that all could be without some kind of healing. There is no doubt that we all have the ability to recover ourselves.

It's an offering from your guides that will aid you in using it as a part of you. For those who haven't connected to The Universal Life Force, which transcends the duality of existence Healing is an essential element of spiritual development.

There is no healing for your body by doing energy-based work. Instead you are connecting to your Universal Life Force Energy. It's a method of increasing your connection with Universal Energy. Universal Energy. All you require is access Universal Life Force Energy and an open mind.

The power of the universe can heal any disease If you let it. If you have your systems of energy in disarray and illness is a result, it develops. Spiritual experts can alter your internal mechanism and tune it up to the ideal frequency of vibration. This is the procedure we follow when we fix an instrument: we balance the tuners by using another cord. Spiritual energy refers to peace, harmony, love and happiness. The methods that are taught within the program "Spiritual Healing" could be used to utilize spiritual guides energy or personal energy into your everyday life.

Chapter 16: Understanding Psychic Empaths

There are many kinds of empaths that specialize in a specific variety of psychic abilities. The empath's sensitivity to earth energy is called geomancy. This ability can be used to douse, detect water underground, or weather forecasting. The capability of psychics to gather impressions from a variety of things is called psychometry. It is often utilized by law enforcement agencies when investigating criminals who are not obvious or vicious.

Claircognizance is an exceptional ability that the empath knows precisely what actions to adopt or what actions to take in any particular situation particularly during emergencies or crisis.They are calm, confident and calm, causing all in their vicinity to behave in the same manner.

Some empaths detect spirits and communicate with them, thereby making them mediums. Some people are able to heal themselves by observing the problems of others and helping them in transmuting energy. They are also able to assist others to heal emotional injuries. Certain empaths are able to communicate with nature as well as through animals. Another unusual ability is precognition, which is where psychic empaths are able to discern events or issues that are at the edge of occurring.

Empaths possess a very strong intuition, also known as a sixth sense, which appears to be an naturally derived extension of empathy. However, as was previously mentioned they often cost a lot for their abilities. They are frequently criticized and often misunderstood. They also may be the subject of hurtful and snide remarks for their words. Empaths are extremely sensitive to their surroundings. This can cause physical discomfort and bizarre allergies that conventional medical professionals can't recognize.

Although their skills and talents are important but they're not all-knowing. Their abilities might not be functioning fully all the all the time, and they're not able to be able to cure every illness or disease within the human race.

The History of Psychic Empaths

The psyche has played a significant role in the history of mankind since the beginning of the civilization. Priestesses, priests, seers and mystics were all employed by various religions prior to the introduction of Christianity.

The Bible includes a variety of psychic seers, such as Samuel, Gad, and Amos. Samuel is the only one to identify the donkey of King Saul. Gad served as David's private psychic medium, and Amos was instructed to quit Judah and to pursue his prophetic powers outside Kingdom by Amaziah.

It is believed that the Greek Oracle of Delphi is one of the most famous names in the field of ancient psychics. It was not a real person; instead, it was a desk chair occupied by the most beautiful women in Delphi. She was able to interpret data directly from Apollo The God who is the God of Light and Truth without having to consult anyone else. The warm springs of the Delphi region helped in enhancing her visions. It is believed that the priests at Ra at Memphis were popular seers in the ancient times of Egypt. In Assyria oracles were identified as nabu, meaning "announce" and "call."

In the French Renaissance, Nostradamus became an internationally renowned seer. His pronouncements are widely known throughout the globe and have been printed on paper ever since they were first written.

The Spiritualist Movement began and expanded during the late nineteenth century at the time that the solar system Neptune came to light (a discovery that governed psychics). The time was when many psychics thrived, including Edgar Cayce, Daniel Dunglas Home along with Madame Blavatsky.

Empathic psychics have been on through the Earth since the very beginning of the human race. But it was not until the 1970s and the 1980s that psychic abilities of empathetic were differentiated from other psychic abilities.

How Empaths Feel

Because empaths are very sensitive to the energetic fields around them, they are often trapped in inner tension and conflict. If your sympathetic side is at its peak You may experience a sense of feeling of nervousness, or like you are experiencing an electrical shock running throughout your body. Then, you experience an explosion of emotions.

Empaths can sense what people around them feel joy, sadness as well as fear and pain. They also sense the energy at work or in a restaurant. It's not a great energy all the times. This is why EMs do not always feel relaxed in some environments or with certain people.

I can still remember the time when my empathy was at its best. I could sense the emotions of people in physical pain.

Then there was another time nearer to where I am today where my gift to read auras was at the highest level which allowed me to sense absolutely all people's thoughts, emotions and pain as they moved through. It was a process of learning from me to figure out how to manage my talent. If their aura is showing anything evident that is difficult for me to miss, I observe a person's aura only when they ask for it.

If you're experiencing a difficult day, you should identify if the issue that's driving you mad or stressed is due to you, or if you're simply absorbing other people's stress.

How Empaths Gain Information

The exact nature of psychic or empathic abilities is still unclear. Numerous theories have been put forward to try and discover the mechanisms behind them However, none could be considered to be conclusive. There are many kinds of empaths however, not all have a single talent. Certain people are able to use various psychic abilities together to create an "mega" psychic capability.

People who are empathic could, for instance, get data by just touching someone or object with their psychometric skills. Their ability to empathize analyses the data and generates emotions. The empaths' clairaudience the ability to see, and other abilities can also assist them in processing the data they are receiving.

As psychic empaths continue to evaluate their own process and decide whether they're working in the realm of empathic ability or an array of abilities It could be difficult for them to discern the results they're getting. It requires a lot of patience and effort to assess every skill that could be tested. But once you've set an established baseline that you've established, it's much easier to see the ways in which your own psychic ability is interconnected and how the skills you have work and interrelate.

Open Up Your Inner Talents

There are many ways to developing your inner talent. I thought that putting this plan on the table could help you in creating a list of the activities needed to reach your goals.

Start meditative practice. The faster you can complete this task the more effective. Because you'll be required to learn new ideas to enable you to attain your maximum potential while contemplating, I think professional assistance is better than trying it yourself. The reason behind this is that it's much easier to say than do. If you're trying to accomplish something by yourself it could mean you miss an amazing learning experience. A lot of people attempt to meditate on their own, but then fail because they cannot make it past the first attempt that makes it difficult to concentrate. In the course of a retreat, you'll be taught how important it is to take this seriously, and how it can aid you in opening your psychic abilities. These is where your psychic abilities are located.

The reason you should know this is to ensure that you will be able to recognize your clients' problems without spending all day talking.If you are aware of the Chakras ability to help, you'll be than able to help people who are seeking your help.

Take time to be in the natural surroundings. To begin, write down the things that have helped you ease into your day. Meditation can help by calming your mind. To become a great psychic, you must be at the present moment in your life. If you're too obsessed with the world of commerce, you'll overlook the ways nature cares for. This is crucial. It helps in feeling compassionate and being in a state of peace with oneself, each of these are essential for anyone who wants to give spiritual direction to other people.

Try practicing Clairvoyance in your daily life. You may be wondering what you can do to achieve this. Clairvoyance is simply "clear vision." This means that you should simplify your life and get back to basic. Clairvoyance is simply the ability to feel and visualize. It is a common ability for psychics and practicing visualization is essential. Take a deep breath and close your eyes for a while to achieve this. If you're feeling low Try to imagine something that makes you feel happy and productive. Keep your eyes on the end objective. Look at it. Be aware of it, and the most important thing is to live it. If you're unsure of you're trying to accomplish This will help you understand it better and motivate you whenever you fail in your judgement. You can't always be correct but you can still learn by imagining those instances when you're wrong to learn from them to ensure that in the future your predictions and your assessments are more accurate.

- Learn to be grounded. Many people see life as a sequence of events that occur to them. They believe that their circumstances and the environment they reside in determine their fate however this isn't the case. The most important moments in life are created through energies (prophecies) which are the reason people who don't feel grounded tend to dwell on the past or fret regarding the future. When you practice yoga, for instance the hands are placed in a particular manner to keep you at a level during your workout. If you're not performing yoga, you need to achieve that balance within yourself.

Conclusion

What do I know to confirm that mindreading is a real thing? I can read minds. It's as easy as that. If my kids want something, I know when they're asking. I'm ready to respond and handle their daily lives effectively due to my feelings of empathy for my children. Perhaps they'll reflect the same behavior in their lives and be able to read minds. I can read the thoughts of my spouse and know that I know what's about to be said since I'm in the same place as my partner and I feel empathy that has been cultivated over many years.

Do I have the ability to read someone else's mind?

Yes, I am able to. The knowledge I gain of the world through reading or travel helps me gain a better knowledge of the different circumstances. I can gaze at someone's eyes and feel their feelings. This is why it's natural to allow the mirror neurons take over. If you'd like to learn this ability, keep in mind the order you have to complete it in:

Clear your mind and make it open to their thoughts

Take your subject's gaze in the face. Learn to read the eyes of your subject

Look away or not into their eyes . Take in their feelings

Are there shady characters in the field of mind-reading?

Of course , there are however, don't be one. The art of mind-reading is a talent that must always be utilized for positive outcomes. Empathy can help you get there, but it is also a way to fix things. Being able to enter into the mind of someone else is a duty and, once you recognize the immenseness of the potential, you could utilize your brain reading skills to turn negative things into profitable initiatives.

You can bring a change in how people see things. You can convince and aid when you're in situations that are extremely difficult. There are so many people who use the catchy phrase "I understand what you're feeling" that it's started to lose its meaning. When you make the effort to calm your mind and pay attention to others' thoughts, you can see the importance of this phrase and it can be helpful in other ways, other than through platitudes. This is when you'll have been through mental reading, and all the benefits that it could do to everyone who are around you.

If you happen to encounter an intersection with someone you don't know, try it. Take a look at them and start a conversation that you are sure that person will react to. Look away and try to get inside their thoughts to understand what's happening. This helps you grow as a person and also helps you become more aware of others' emotions. This is a great thing in and of itself. If you can assist them make their thinking more beneficial and positive for them, it's more rewarding, however, you must to be open to their ideas and understand how to take their thoughts into your own mind. If your mind is overloaded with your own thoughts, this will not occur.

The story for the stranger has been offered as a way to understand. It is one of the most powerful tools minds can utilize. In my particular instance I was waiting for a bus with an unknown person. I could tell by their agitated expressions that the person in question was not a native of this area. I said a kind word and looked him in the eyes. What I saw as I turned away was awe-inspiring to some extent. It was like going back in time and finding yourself in that same situation in which you've lost your mom and you're standing alone in the park, worried that you do not know where she might be.

What was the purpose of this? I made a new acquaintance one who required to get to know someone to feel at ease in a city that was unfamiliar to him. It's one of the advantages that you can enjoy when you take the time to listen to minds.

www.ingramcontent.com/pod-product-compliance
Lightning Source LLC
Chambersburg PA
CBHW050401120526
44590CB00015B/1782